Modern Sports Writers:
a collection of prose

Edited by John Byrne
Formerly Head of English,
Ashton-under-Lyne Sixth Form College

Batsford Academic and Educational Ltd   London

© Introduction and commentaries John Byrne 1982
First published 1982

All rights reserved. No part of this publication
may be reproduced, in any form or by any means,
without permission from the Publisher

Typeset by Tek-Art Ltd, London SE20
and printed in Great Britain by
Billing & Son Ltd
London, Guildford & Worcester
for the publishers
Batsford Academic and Educational Ltd,
an imprint of B.T. Batsford Ltd,
4 Fitzhardinge Street
London W1H 0AH

ISBN 0 7134 4303 0

Contents

Introduction	5
Cricket	9
Soccer	45
Rugby Union	73
Rugby League	99
Golf	105
Lawn Tennis	143
Acknowledgments	169
Index of Authors	171
Index of Titles	173

Introduction

Much excellent prose writing on the subject of sport has been a prominent feature of modern and contemporary literature. The object of this anthology has been to select some of it to help to satisfy a natural interest (for girls as well as boys), and to indicate ways in which some of the chosen passages may suggest approaches for original creative writing on sport and other themes, particularly for "O" Level Essay work. The extracts begin with Bernard Darwin and Sir Neville Cardus, the initiators of a new kind of literary journalism to whom most sports writers of today have freely and gladly acknowledged their debt.

Sir Neville Cardus enlivened and deepened his sports' writing by illustrations and parallels from other arts — "the approximation of the arts". He spoke of an entire gallery of characters being on view in the 1973 cricket season, "classic, impressionist, pre-Raphaelite, surrealist and so on". Clive Lloyd was "classic and romantic and spectacular", and as a "creative batsman" could survive comparison with the most original in any age of the game's history. A "mixture of tradition and latest surrealism" could be found in an innings by George Gunn which could make Cardus think of Louis Armstrong playing in the Philharmonic Orchestra while a symphony of Mozart was being performed and suddenly improvising to suit his mood of the moment.

Such is the flavour of Cardus, along with his insistence that "the game is still rich in characters".

Bernard Darwin's prose reflected his enthusiasm for the game as writer and player (he was made a C.B.E.), his whimsicality (with apt quotations from his Dickens treasury) and the orderliness and urbanity of his style. He had a fine gift for portraiture, as in his studies on Vardon and Sarazen, but could write an equally fine appraisal of a new hero — "That Small Colossus: Hogan at Carnoustie".

Introduction

Many other engaging personalities are met, and a large variety of styles and methods of literary presentation encountered.

The effortless and economical style of Henry Longhurst can open many doors for the young writer. He also writes of sport in a larger perspective, a salutary corrective for the over-intellectualising of much sports' writing. His sense of humour and love of the eccentric in life and sport made him a much loved figure on both sides of the Atlantic.

The fresh and precise writing of John Arlott, always a seeker after the unique word, is a tribute to his great knowledge of sport and his very acute observation. This is in contrast with the blurred and emotive jargon of so much popular sports' journalism. Like Cardus, he is a master of the illustrative anecdote.

Geoffrey Green, another in our gallery of enthusiasts, had for his football travels a maxim — "Every day is Christmas Day". This shows through in the freshness of his writing which is always illuminated by his stored impressions of Turin, Brazil or Wembley. He has a great appreciation of character in the game and writes of Bobby Charlton's "flowing skills and modesty, his integrity and example to others, both in and off the field".

Pat Ward-Thomas evokes the special qualities of golf courses and golf holes that have brought pleasure and apprehension to players all over the world, and has expressed better than anyone the great love that a master golfer and very fine personality can inspire in his own generation and beyond.

The excitement and glamour of Wimbledon have been well caught by David Gray and Rex Bellamy.

Peter Dobereiner can better than anyone give us the urbane, intelligent discussion of golfing themes that would illuminate locker-room and clubhouse talk, with his often very original ideas.

A course on narrative and short-story writing could well be illustrated by examples from the literature of sport, the flowing style and wit of P.G. Wodehouse being pre-eminent in the short-story field.

The possibilities of sport as a subject for humorous writing have led to much outstanding work, and some of the terms invented by notable authors have passed into the language, those on "gamesmanship" having world-wide connotation, and the permutations of "Coarse" being used in contexts other than sport.

Introduction

Other writers have their own special contribution to make of style and expression, but always they bring to their work the quality of gusto and enthusiasm, the deep love for the game that is their abiding interest, and it is hoped that the young writer will also be offering ideas on subjects meaningful to himself.

Practice in subjects appropriate to the 30-minute type of essay used as part of comprehension tests will be necessary, but the majority of the suggested subjects will be for the one-hour essay paper. A thematic approach can often be successful and can be used for extended writing — Classic Encounters, Sport as Drama, Gamesmanship, Sporting Venues — Lords, Old Trafford, St Andrews, Wimbledon, Wembley, Anfield. Subjects suggested by the extracts can be useful — Sir Neville Cardus on George Gunn can lead to many appraisals of "Characters"; Alan Gibson on Jessop, the "Croucher", to Nicknames and their Recipients; Geoffrey Moorhouse on "The Roses Match", to A Local "Derby"; Bernard Darwin on "The Links of Eiderdown", to Sporting Dreams.

General sporting subjects which can also be made to fit themes of a more general nature, involving description, argument, reportage, nostalgia, are manifold.

Before The Match, A Tight Finish, An Embarrassing Experience in Sport, Explain why you loyally follow a club that is having a poor season, Putting the Clock Back — an old-fashioned sporting occasion, Explain one of your favourite games to a non-player, Tell the story in sport of a disability successfully overcome, Re-create an exciting twentieth-century sporting occasion in which you would have liked to have played a part, The Trials and Triumphs of Learning a New Game, My Sporting Image (and me), Breakfast Dreams of Sport on a Saturday Morning, and the subsequent reality, "If only . . . " in sport, Sporting Sounds, Describe the sporting recollection you will remember longest, Describe a sporting event the result of which has been important to you, bringing out the atmosphere and your own feelings, A Flooded Ground, "Break-Time" Sport at School, Finding an Old "Real Tennis" Racquet, The Rewards and Disadvantages of Sporting Fame, Are you in favour of the Olympic Games?, Visiting a Sporting Hero at Home, Do you believe that sport is taken too seriously?, Sporting Ideas for Helping Local Charities, Would you have preferred more coaching at sport?, Our Park, its Sports and Personalities, Which sporting hero or heroine would you most like to have been?, Crowd

Introduction

Behaviour, The Appeal of Old-Fashioned Sporting Equipment, A Sporting Personality and the reasons he has impressed you — describe his appearance to open the local supermarket and give an account of the speech he made.

Lively narrative on sporting subjects can be very stimulating and can be written as if for the School Magazine or local radio.

A subject could be the re-visiting by a sporting hero of a place that he knew as a child, and the description of his thoughts and feelings. "Deep Sentimental Value" could be the story of a sportsman's loss of something which he has treasured over many years. "The Missing Forward" could be a mystery story. A new episode (in acceptable English) of "Roy of the Rovers". You choose a sporting photograph or print and write a story in which the scene depicted plays a part. "The weakest link" — a sports story. Continue the story: "When I saw the team sheet . . . ".

There are many excellent writers on sport not featured in this anthology. Of English writers find out something about "Crusoe" (Robertson-Glasgow) and Patric Dickinson.

American writing about sport has much to offer, especially in the stories of Ernest Hemingway and Ring Lardner and the essays and articles by Herbert Warren Wind, Charles Price, Grantland Rice and George Plimpton.

But most of all, something new by yourself!

Cricket

Sir Neville Cardus

GEORGE GUNN

Sir Neville Cardus (1890-1975) was for many years Cricket Correspondent of the *Manchester Guardian*. He also wrote music criticism for the same paper.

He saw cricket as an art-form which expressed traditional values, and, with romantic imagery and a rich fund of nostalgia and recollection, he made the sports' pages of the *Manchester Guardian* compelling reading.

Some have thought his early style overwrought, and because of his musical and literary comparisons, over-allusive. But, when his medium is firmly under control, he can evoke the magic of the game, with its "characters", as no-one else can.

Here he writes about George Gunn of Nottinghamshire. Those who have condemned Cardus's social viewpoint as anachronistic cannot have been thinking of this piece on George Gunn, a free spirit and a "creative" cricketer who expressed his personality through the game.

GEORGE GUNN

George Gunn was one of the characters of cricket, a rare 'original', to use the old term. We cannot discuss his style of play, his technique, in the abstract, as a thing separable from the man himself in all his humours. For our delight, George Gunn could do things which with other men would have seemed foolish and vain. We must try to remember him always in terms of his personal touch; we must get him permanently into a scene, frame him like a picture. I see him now, and for ever, as I once saw him on a hot July day at Trent Bridge when Macdonald was great and formidable. Along the earth ran Macdonald silently, curving his sinuous beautiful wrist. George Gunn walked down the pitch to the fastest balls, and played them away for intimate singles, with time to spare. Suddenly Macdonald dropped one short;

it flew upwards savagely. And George Gunn calmly reached it with his bat as it was flashing near his head; he hit the ball straight to the earth, 'swatted' it like a man killing a disagreeable wasp. The ball spun round and round on the grass at George Gunn's feet. When the whirling motions had ceased, and the ball was quite still, George Gunn gently patted it down the wicket back to the bowler, who, had he been anybody but Macdonald, would have dropped with surprise.

Another picture—and if it is not true it ought to be; it certainly observes the highest order of truth, which is truth of character. A sweltering day at Edgbaston; a lovely stretch of turf on which a novice at batting was at liberty to make runs for the asking. George Gunn came in with Whysall to begin the Nottinghamshire innings. He wore a white panama hat for the occasion. In a quarter of an hour he scored twenty runs by impertinent little cuts from Howell through the crowded slips. He pulled a noble break-back off his middle stump for four. Then, without a warning sign, he daintily returned a half-volley to the bowler, a gift direct into the hand. When he returned to the pavilion his captain said: 'Good heavens, George, what were you doing to get out to a ball like that?' And George Gunn replied: 'Too hot, sir.'

A year or two before the war, Nottinghamshire had to tackle a huge score by Yorkshire. They had nothing to hope for or play for but a draw. George Gunn batted six hours and scored a hundred runs not out. The Yorkshire bowlers waxed sarcastic at George Gunn's slowness. Nottinghamshire followed on; the score-sheet of their second innings can be seen in Mr. A.W. Shelton's fine collection of relics and memorials in the Trent Bridge pavilion. Nobody in Nottinghamshire's second innings made double figures, the final score was Nottinghamshire some 138 for five; George Gunn's share was 108 not out, cut and driven and coaxed and cajoled in less than two hours.

He was the wittiest batsman that ever lived; his bat was a swift rapier not for warfare but just to tickle the ribs. He played the game for fancy's sake; he never knew where the imp of his genius was going to take him. He could stonewall, but with what a relish of the irony of it!—because he knew that he could as easily be hitting boundaries. And he knew that the bowlers knew. Often he allowed a wretched long-hop to bowl his wicket down; he would pick up the fallen stump, and put it back into its hole, and give it a helpful knock on th top with his bat before departing to the pavilion. But as often would he send the finest ball of the match to the rails by a stroke as impudent as a coxcomb. At Old Trafford a year or two ago he won a match by himself against Macdonald on a fiery pitch. The other Nottinghamshire batsmen ducked their heads helplessly, and suffered many bruises. George Gunn was not touched once by Macdonald's flashing pace; either he journeyed forth from his crease and pushed a ball forward as it bounced on the half-volley, or he waited far back on his stumps until the ball was passing him shoulder high, when he flicked it between the slips to an inch. Sibbles sent him an over-tossed length; he drove it to the on, lazily, at arm's length so to say—a reclining stroke. He did not run, because he expected the ball to go over the boundary; but it stopped an inch or two within the field. Sibbles's next ball was entirely different in pitch and direction, but George Gunn drove it to the on exactly to the same place where the other hit had travelled. This time, though, the ball was four all the way. I have seen him tease one of the finest fieldsmen in the world for hours, playing a ball a yard or so to the right of him, then to the left of him, then in front of him, then suddenly knocking the man almost off his feet by a cover-drive so splendid that it opened classical doors on the game, and let us see the image of William Gunn himself. George Gunn could invest himself in armour as well as in motley.

Years ago he happened to be in Australia for his health when the England eleven were beaten in a Test match by a new and devastating googly bowler. George Gunn was asked to play in the subsequent Test match. He scattered the googly bowler's attack to the winds; he pounced on the spin, and drove far and wide; then, when the googly bowler dropped the inevitable short length, George Gunn cut it to ribbons, as the saying goes. He scored a hundred, and exposed the limitations of the new terror, and when he came back to the pavilion he threw his bat with a thud on to a locker and, indicating the googly man with a jerk of his thumb through the window, he said: 'He's a Saturday afternoon bowler, that's what he is, Saturday afternoon!' There was no good or bad bowling for George Gunn; it all depended on his mood.

I fancy he arranged his centuries as he arranged all his pleasures, on the spur of the moment, according to whether he felt like it. Once he argued to me in his own humorous accents, that 'what cricket needed nowadays was brighter batting'. The public, it seemed, deserved some consideration. After delivering this homily, George Gunn proceeded (at Bradford) to bat for four hours for 48. I have no doubt he

Cricket

did it on purpose, knowing that I would see the joke. His mastery over all sorts of bowling was remarkable; never did he seem to be attending to any tune not his own. His range of strokes apparently included them all, ancient and modern, with, of course, variations of his own thrown in to lend savour. His bat might well have been an extension of his right arm, with the funny-bone in it. It was a tactile bat, a bat that seemed to 'feel', to vibrate to, every stroke. George Gunn's cricket possessed a quality, a sensibility, which I can only call 'touch'. Even an ordinary forward defensive push by George Gunn caused you to get a sense that some current of his personality had run down the bat's handle, through the blade, into the ball. He had a lovable way of tapping a ball through the slips as he was beginning his run for the single. And as he sauntered along the pitch he would pat turf with his bat.

He was a man who enjoyed the flavours and significances of things private and intimate. There was always a little comedy, or rather a conceit, going on in George Gunn's cricket. His strokes were quips and paradoxes and wise saws. Because there was sense in the chaff continually. George Gunn's style at bottom was classical in its soundness and beauty; no handsomer cover-drives and cuts than his were seen in his day. He learned to play cricket in its greatest period; and at the age of fifty he was, with Hobbs and Woolley, one of the complete batsmen of our own period. He was an instinctive cricketer: he was related to the immortal William Gunn*, and did not know how he came into his heritage; he was born a great batsman. I have never heard him indulge in theories about batsmanship. I can imagine if anybody talked to him about the science of the game, he would answer much as my Uncle Toby answered old Shandy (I quote from memory, and make the necessary adaptation): 'And have you never considered the theory of cause and effect in these things? 'No more than my horse!' O rare George Gunn, the game is poorer now that, at last, the comedy of your long career is finished.

From *Cardus on Cricket*, by Sir Neville Cardus, published by Souvenir Press Ltd.

---

* Uncle to George Gunn, and like him an opening batsman for Notts.

John Arlott

WHEN LAKER WALKED TALL ON PARK AVENUE

John Arlott was Cricket Correspondent on the *Guardian*, and commentator on wine, for many years. His literary style is meticulous and he took great pleasure in trying to characterise the styles of famous batsmen and bowlers.

He enjoyed fame as a cricket commentator on radio and T.V.

The newspaper article here was one of a series, published in the *Guardian* in April 1980, called "The Summer of '48". In the series, John Arlott recalled some of the "great moments in past English Test trials".

WHEN LAKER WALKED TALL ON PARK AVENUE

The English cricket spectator is at heart partisan. He relishes rivalry, the older and the more local the better. For that reason the technically finest domestic cricket matches, Test Trials, rouse little excitement and rarely attract appreciable crowds. Thus only a few people have watched some outstanding performances.

In 1923 Maurice Tate, hitherto primarily a batsman, but a run of the mill county off spinner, suddenly emerged, at the age of 28, as the greatest of all fast-medium bowlers. The change was bred out of sheer frustration. At the end of July 1922 he had bowled long and unavailingly to that obdurate left-hander, Philip Mead, when, from his ordinary off-spinner's run he had released a faster — much faster — ball that bowled him. He began 1923 in that new style; there was no touring side in England that summer and so two Test Trials were played and Maurice Tate bowled himself into both of them.

Nearer today, in the Worcester Trial of 1974, Geoffrey

Cricket

Boycott scored a century in each innings by a technique as virtually flawless as even he has ever achieved. It is sometimes forgotten, too, that, in the same match, John Edrich, without a mistake, almost emulated him with 106 and 95. Yet it's doubtful if any of these performances were more outstanding than Jim Laker's in the Test Trial of 1950. He had been blamed — and, indeed, had been inclined to blame himself — for England's failure to beat Bradman's Australians in the Headingley Test of 1948. In fact, though, the late decision to leave out the second spinner and the missing of seven chances (three from Bradman off Laker) were powerful contributory factors.

His talent was unquestionable. During the war, stories had come back to England of the young off-spinner playing Services cricket in Egypt whose spin was such that the batsman at the non-striking end heard the ball buzz as it left his fingers. With peace, post-war cricketing England saw him, like Trueman, a year or two later, as something of a symbol of the new age of the English game. Indeed, he was chosen for the arduous 1947-48 tour of West Indies after only 14 first-class matches.

So, although finger spin is traditionally associated with wide and deep experience of the craft, he had to take some technical short cuts. He had, though, never compromised in the matter of spin or length. After Headingley he was dropped from the team for the fifth Test; was not taken on the South African tour of the following winter and was chosen for only one of the four New Zealand Tests of 1949.

So he had a place to win when he was picked for the 1950 Test Trial at Bradford. That is one of the most honest cricket pitches in the world. In normal conditions it is a fine wicket for stroke making; but, after rain, drying conditions will stir it into a true "sticky"; as both the 1948 Australian, and the 1950 West Indian sides discovered to their alarm in their games with Yorkshire.

The two teams included five of the young University batsmen — Hubert Doggart, Peter May, John Dewes and David Sheppard from Cambridge, and Donald Carr of Oxford, who had been making so many runs on good wickets, especially those at Fenners. The nominated twelfth man was the Hampshire opener, Neville Rogers, always a skilful player of off-spin and who, four years later carried his bat for MCC against Surrey at Lord's when Laker was at his most destructive. Although two of the original selections dropped out, however, replacements were drafted in, and Rogers remained twelfth man.

Cricket

May 31, 1950 was a chilly day in Bradford with a scattered crowd taking shelter from the wind on the Park Avenue ground, only five miles from Shipley, where Jim Laker was born. He had been noticed and coached by Yorkshire as a promising batsman for Saltaire before the war but, after he left to join the army at the age of eighteen, he never returned to the county. Now, his father and mother were dead; he was established in the south; and an elderly aunt was his only remaining relative in the district.

It was argued afterwards that, if the match was to be of any value to the selectors, the pitch should have been covered, or England, instead of the Rest, should have batted. The wicket, though, had been left open to the rain and now it was drying under the influence of wind and fitful sunshine; while the England captain, Norman Yardley, could also regard himself as on trial. So, lacking any instructions from the selectors to the contrary, he put the Rest in to bat.

Jim Laker went out to look at the pitch, recognised its character, and knew precisely what he had to do. Yardley kept on Trevor Bailey and Alec Bedser long enough to dispose of David Sheppard before he called up Laker, who set an attacking leg-side field, went round the wicket and pitched length and line at once.

Never a demonstrative cricketer, he was now in his element and at his most noncommital. Tongue in cheek, he strolled back to his mark at his characteristic constabulary gait; looked up to the sky as he turned and then jogged the approach he used artfully to vary, constantly changing the number of steps so as, often, to defeat the batsman's timing.

Although Laker was a master of flight, he understood only too well that he did not need it now. He gave the ball little or no air, the batsmen no time to move out to him. Only Don Kenyon shaped remotely convincingly at him. The young men relied on the forward defensive push, but it was not enough. The ball leapt and turned spitefully. In his first over Hubert Doggart and Peter May were picked up at short-leg and still not a run had been scored from Laker when Donald Carr went in the same way.

Faced with a dilemma when Eric Bedser came in at number six, he could hardly fail to give his county team mate a friendly "one off the mark" and wheeled up a full toss. Eric carefully pushed it to mid-on where his brother Alec had thoughtfully moved four or five yards deeper than necessary, and took a single. Kenyon, deceived by a ball which went with the arm, was caught at the wicket by Godfrey Evans;

Eric Bedser lbw to one which hurried through; Dick Spooner and Bob Berry bowled "through the gate," before Fred Trueman inside-edged a single and then was stumped off the returning Alec Bedser. To complete his morning Laker picked up a savage drive to catch and bowl Les Jackson.

Ten minutes before lunch the Rest were out for 27, the lowest total ever made in a representative match. For an hour and a half of perfect and hostile spin bowling, Laker's figures were 14 overs; 12 maidens; two runs; eight wickets; bettered statistically only by the nine for two of a certain Gideon Elliott, once described as "the fastest and straightest bowler in Australia" for Victoria against Tasmania in 1857-58.

The local boy had made good. No one from his youth was there on a working-day morning to share the moment with him: but the England team and the Rest Batsmen who had been his victims formed up to applaud him into the pavilion, with unmistakably whole-hearted admiration.

In the afternoon Len Hutton played an innings of superb virtuosity against the pace of Len Jackson and Fred Trueman, the cut of Alec Bedser, the leg-spin of Roly Jenkins and the slow left-arm of Bob Berry. Although the wicket had eased a little, the spun ball still turned sharply but Hutton was at his masterly best, playing in complete sympathy with the break, seeming, indeed, to harness it to his stroke. Reggie Simpson made a typically poised 26 off the fast bowlers; Bill Edrich a determined 46; but Hutton's 85, before he became Trueman's only wicket of the match, was a masterpiece.

Bob Berry's five for 73 took him into the first Test but could not save the game for the Rest. Eric Bedser made a capable 30 and Spooner 20 but Eric Hollies, with six for 28, bowled them out a second time, and before lunch on the second day, England had won by an innings and 89 runs.

After that performance Laker could hardly be left out of the first Test against West Indies but his one wicket for 86 after injuring his hand while batting when Hollies and Berry bowled England to a win on the dusty pitch at Old Trafford, was not enough to keep him in the side. Overwhelmed by the batting of Everton Weekes, Frank Worrell, Clyde Walcott and Alan Rae, England were heavily beaten in the three remaining Tests.

No one who played with or against him would dispute that Jim Laker was the finest off-spinner, certainly of his own time, probably of any. Yet, amazingly, while England played ninety-nine Tests between his first and last appearances he took part in only forty-six of them: went only once to Australia and once to South Africa.

His nineteen wickets against Australia at Old Trafford which surely will never be equalled and another "all ten" against them for Surrey, of course, lay still six years into the future from Bradford. Then, in 1956, he took 46 Australian Test wickets at 9.60 and virtually won the series by his own efforts.

He probably took equal pleasure from his figures in Australia in 1958-59. A number of the Australians believed that the English pitches of 1953 and 1956 had been "cooked" for him; and several declared they would murder him on their own pitches. He took immense tactical thought before he went on that tour. Although the cruelly arthritic finger which eventually ended his career prevented him playing at Adelaide in an England side beaten by four matches to none, he bowled more overs, took more wickets and had a better Test average than any other English bowler. That gave him immense, though unspoken, satisfaction.

Reminded of the Bradford eight for two, he recalls with a wry grin the question of a local reporter: "Are these your best bowling figures, Mr Laker?"

From the *Guardian*, 23 April 1980.

Harold Pinter

MEMORIES OF CRICKET

Harold Pinter has an established reputation as one of Britain's leading playwrights.

He has always taken a great interest in cricket, and its London venues, and told in an interview that in 1944, when houses in London were often evacuated because of flying bombs, he always took his cricket bat with him.

The article "Memories of Cricket" consists of disparate recollections.

MEMORIES OF CRICKET

Hardstaff and Simpson at Lords. Notts versus Middlesex. 1946 or 1947. After lunch. Keeton and Harris had opened for Notts. Keeton swift, exact, interested; Harris Harris. Harris stonewalled five balls in the over for no particular reason and hit the sixth for six, for no particular reason. Keeton and Harris gave Notts a fair start. Stott, at number three, smacked the ball hard, was out in the early afternoon. Simpson joined Hardstaff. Both very upright in their stance. They surveyed the field, surveyed themselves, began to bat.

The sun was strong, but calm. They settled into the afternoon, no hurry, all in order. Hardstaff clipped to mid-wicket. They crossed. Simpson guided the ball between midoff and the bowler. They crossed. Their cross was a trot, sometimes a walk, they didn't need to run. They placed their shots with precision, they knew where they were going. Bareheaded. Hardstaff golden. Simpson dark. Hardstaff offdrove, silently. Simpson to deep square leg. Simpson cut. Hardstaff cut, finer. Simpson, finer. The slips, Robertson, Bennett, attentive. Hardstaff hooked, immaculate, no sound. They crossed, and back. Deep square leg in the heat after it. Jim

Sims on at the pavilion end with leg breaks. Hardstaff wristed him into the covers. Simpson to fine leg. Two. Sims twisting. Hardstaff wristed him into the covers, through the covers, fielder wheeling, for four. Quite unhurried. Seventy in 90 minutes. No explosions. Batsmanship. Hardstaff caught at slip, off Sims.

Worrell and Weekes at Kingston on Thames. 1950. The Festival. Headley had flicked, showed what had been and what remained of himself, from the Thirties. Worrell joined Weekes with an hour to play. Gladwin and Jackson bowling. Very tight, very crisp, just short of a length, jolting, difficult. Worrell and Weekes scored 90 before close of play. No sixes, nothing off the ground. Weekes smashed, red-eyed, past cover, smashed to long leg, at war, met Gladwin head on, split midwicket in two, steel. Worrell wanted to straight drive to reach his 50. Four men at the sight screen to stop him. He straight drove, pierced them, reached his 50. Gladwin bowled a stinging ball, only just short, on middle and leg. Only sensible course was to stop it. Worrell jumped up, both feet off, slashed it from his stomach, square cut for four, boundary first bounce.

MCC versus Australians. Lords 1948. Monday. On the Saturday the Australians had plastered the MCC bowling, Barnes 100, Bradman just short. On Monday morning Miller hit Laker for five sixes into the Tavern. The Australians passed 500 and declared. The weather darkened. MCC 30 minutes batting before lunch. The Australians came into the field chucking the ball hard at each other, broad, tall, sure. Hutton and Robertson took guard against Lindwall and Miller. Robertson caught Tallon off Miller. Lindwall and Miller very fast. The sky black. Edrich caught Tallon off Miller. Last ball before lunch. MCC 20 for 2.

After lunch the Australians, arrogant, jocular, muscular, larking down the pavilion steps. They waited, hurling the ball about, eight feet tall. Two shapes behind the pavilion glass. Frozen before emerging a split second. Hutton and Compton. We knew them to be the two greatest English batsmen. Down the steps together, out to the middle. They played. The Australians were quieter, wary, tight. Bradman studied them. They stayed together for an hour before Compton was out, and M.P. Donnelly, and Hutton, and the Australians walked home.

First Test at Trent Bridge. The first seven in the English batting order: Hutton, Washbrook, Edrich, Compton, Hardstaff, Barnett, Yardley. They'll never get them out, I said.

Cricket

At lunch on the first day, England 78 for 8.
Hutton.
England versus New Zealand 1949. Hutton opened quietly, within himself, setting his day in order. At the first hour England 40 for none, Hutton looking set for a score. Burtt, slow left hand, took the ball at the Nursery end, tossed it up. To his first ball Hutton played a superb square drive to Wallace at deep point. Wallace stopped it. The crowd leaned in. Burtt again. Hutton flowed into another superb square drive to Wallace's right hand. Wallace stopped it. Back to the bowler. Burtt again, up. Hutton, very hard a most brilliant square drive to Wallace's left hand. Wallace stopped it. Back to the bowler. The crowd. Burtt in, bowled. Hutton halfway up the pitch immediately, driving straight. Missed it. Clean bowled. On his heel back to the pavilion.

Hutton was never dull. His bat was part of his nervous system. His play was sculptured. His forward defensive stroke was a complete statement. The handle of his bat seemed electric. Always, for me, a sense of his vulnerability, of a very uncommon sensibility. He never just went through the motions, nothing was glibly arrived at. He was never, for me, as some have defined him, simply a "master technician". He attended to the particular but rarely lost sight of the context in which it took place. But one day in Sydney he hit 37 in 24 minutes and was out last ball before lunch when his bat slipped in hitting a further four, when England had nothing to play for but a hopeless draw, and he's never explained why he did *that*. I wasn't there to see it and probably regret that as much as anything. But I wasn't surprised to hear about it, because every stroke he made surprised me.

I heard about Hutton's 37 on the radio. 7 a.m. Listened every morning of the 1946/47 series. Alan McGilvray talking. Always England six wickets down and Yardley 35 not out. But it was in an Irish kitchen in County Galway that, alone, I heard Edrich and Compton in 1953 clinch the Ashes for England.

Those were the days of Bedser and Wright, Evans, Washbrook and Gimblett, M.P. Donnelly, Smailes and Bowes, A.B. Sellars, Voce and Charley Barnett, S.M. Brown and Jim Sims, Mankad, Mustaq Ali, Athol Rowan, even H.T. Bartlett, even Hammond and certainly Bradman.

One morning at drama school I pretended illness and pale and shaky walked into Gower St. Once round the corner I jumped on a bus and ran into Lords at the Nursery end to see through the terraces Washbrook late cutting for four, the ball skidding towards me. That beautiful evening Compton made 70.

But it was 1950 when G.H.G. Doggart missed Walcott at slip off Edrich and Walcott went on to score 165, Gomez with him. Christiani was a very good fielder. Ramadhin and Valentine had a good season. Hutton scored 202 not out against them and against Goddard bowling breakbacks on a bad wicket at the Oval.

It was 1949 when Bailey caught Wallace blindingly at silly mid on. And when was it I watched Donnelly score 180 for the Gents versus Players? He went down the afternoon with his lightning pulls.

Constantine hitting a six over fine leg into the pavilion. Talk of a schoolboy called May.

From the *Daily Telegraph Magazine*, 16 May 1969.

Ronald Mason

AN OVER OF O'REILLY'S

Ronald Mason was a Civil Servant and then a University Lecturer in Literature. He wrote outstanding biographies of Sir Jack Hobbs and Walter Hammond, and a collection of cricket essays, *Batsman's Paradise*. In addition, he has published a good deal of general work on English Literature. *Sing all a green willow*, from which the following extract is taken, consists of some striking character studies of well-known players of the fairly recent past and a section dealing with some of the celebrated writings about the game.

AN OVER OF O'REILLY'S

The great-hearted pertinacity of this colossal bowler never achieved more signal or symbolic reward than was collected into the confines of one astonishing over in the Manchester Test Match of 1934. O'Reilly's consuming energy never yielded anything but his best endeavours; but the essence of his greatness always seemed perversely called out by the most unpromising conditions, as if he could only give of his fullest glory when in a glowering and justifiable rage. Here he had all he could have asked; Manchester went ironically back on itself that July and offered a grilling inexorable heat-wave, a rock-hard wicket over which the noonday haze flickered and danced, and a captain who, losing the toss, let into the easy slaughterhouse an England batting-order which contained as far down as number seven a batsman who made 100 centuries in first-class cricket and at number ten a batsman who more than once opened the innings for England.

The Australian speed bowlers, Wall and McCabe, were triers rather than penetrators; O'Reilly, seeing the shine go off the ball and the England openers settle in the cooking heat of the July day, cracked his finger-joints impatiently with memories in his mind of the eleven wickets he had taken in the first Test and the pasting that Leyland and Ames had given him in the second. The first episode needed renewal, the second revision and revenge. Meanwhile, Sutcliffe and Walters seemed in no trouble at all.

Sutcliffe was by this time a rooted and unassailable tradition, for ten years at once the anchor of England's hopes and the unruffled pilot of her fortunes. He abode at one end as of right, contemplating every shock or subtlety with his customary brand of good-tempered superiority. At the other end, his elegant and fluent partner, Cyril Walters, made aggressive war on the opening bowlers with the captivating grace that for a few seasons—and they were far too few—made greybeards babble of the lost lovelinesses of Palairet and Spooner.* Walters, with his courtly resource, made every device of attack look inevitable and easy. He had a brooding thoughtful face and a kind of sombre watchfulness of method which translated itself when he positioned himself for his stroke into rhythmic, almost somnambulistic beauty of movement. Not that he sleepwalked; the contrary. He hit the first ball of an earlier Test match crack through the open covers for four, and in the first hour of this one he had plundered eight boundaries, a rude and rough beginning by modern Test Match standards, but worthy of the tradition that any latter-day opening partner of Sutcliffe had perforce to inherit.

Even the arrival of Grimmett and O'Reilly to supplant the opening attackers did not subdue Walters' poised assurance. In an hour he had reached as lovely a fifty as Manchester had seen in a decade of Tests; Sutcliffe, no doubt recalling many similar experiences with the greatest of all his partners, was only just into his 'teens; and the avid drouth of midsummer compelled a stoppage for drinks with the score at 68. It was at this point that somebody (Bradman, I'll bet) noticed that the ball had gone out of shape, presumably in surprise and indignation at the violence of Walters' uncompromising treatment of it; the game was held up while another was obtained to match it as nearly as could be managed; and after the rumours and flurries had been calmed down and the officious bustle died away, Walters prepared equably to resume the cultured flow as O'Reilly, no doubt irritably,

---

* R.H. Spooner ("the most lyrical of cricketers") played for Lancashire from 1899 onwards. Palairet was another very elegant batsman, who played for Somerset.

came plunging up to begin a new over.

He began it as he meant to go on; the first ball was his virulent googly and it spun back at Walters as he came forward to smother it. O'Reilly was always a master of deceitful flight and he hung this one back a trifle, so that Walters' watchful and controlled forward shot was that crucial fraction too early for it. Darling, at forward short-leg, scooped up the catch with clean certainty; the crowd gave Walters their hearty and grateful applause as he retreated, signing himself off after a sweetly characteristic display of beauty and evanescence.

Bob Wyatt, the England captain, first wicket down, was an admirable match in dour aggressiveness for the bowler he had to face. Loving a tough situation, he was equally pleased with what looked like a highly promising one. O'Reilly knew as well as anyone on the field how capable this batsman was of subduing the most varied and hostile attack, and how impervious to weather and fortune was his amiable and equable temperament; and no doubt as he came charging up to bowl him his first ball he permitted himself to attempt the impossible and hate him. However he may have succeeded at that, he effected his prime purpose; the ball pitched on a perfect length on the line of the leg stump, defeated one of the most reliable defensive bats in the game, and knocked the middle stump out of the ground. I have seen somewhere a photograph of Wyatt's wide-eyed surprise, and the ear of the imagination can hear the explosive answering roar of the crowd's dismay.

Infinitely reassuring was the appearance in his place of the great Walter Hammond. The masterful ease of this superb batsman was communicated in his very air and walk, as the crowd rose joyfully to his arrival. Neither he nor anyone else knew that he happened to be in the middle of a dreadful run of Test failures; his Gloucestershire form in this strange season was commanding and productive, and his latest first-class innings was a little matter of 290. (His next was to be 217.) He cocked his cap as he took guard, looked with his customary indolent indifference down the wicket at the bowler, and prepared massively to stop the hat-trick, for which O'Reilly may be confidently presumed to have tried his damnedest.

Reports about what happened next vary; all that is certain is that the ball went for four to fine-leg out of a cloud of dust. One account credits Hammond with a masterly leg-glance; one would like to think this true. Others, and again there is a disturbingly corroborative photograph, accuse him of a desperate snick and a Chinese cut off the inside edge; it does not much matter. Whatever it was, it was four runs. O'Reilly, I imagine, tore most of his remaining hair bodily out of his scalp amid the frenzied yells of all present, and gathered up all his faculties to a supreme concentration of venom in advance of anything he had achieved to date. The next, and fourth, ball of this classic over was accordingly yards and yards faster in the air and off the pitch than flesh and blood had been trained to expect, and it destroyed Hammond's wicket beyond hope of repair before he could assemble a recognizable stroke at all. The fourth roar in five troubled minutes set boats rocking on the Manchester Ship Canal, and the resultant buzz and commotion were such as to distract attention from the perky and bustling arrival of Hendren and his successful endeavours to keep the last two barbed deliveries out of his wicket. 68 for 0 was 72 for 3; and what a three! It was enough to turn the hair grey of anyone but Sutcliffe, aloof and disapproving at the other end.

It is hardly to be believed that after this catastrophic experience England made 627 for nine, but that is what they did. Calm hands papered over the cracks; Hendren made a hundred, Leyland made a hundred, Sutcliffe, Ames, Allen and Verity all got over sixty. Poor O'Reilly bowled 59 overs and they cost 189 all told; but who cares, he got seven wickets and they were all frontline batsmen. Nobody cares what happened to the match, nobody remembers the toil and the frustration and the centuries and the records. But nobody who saw it or read about it will ever forget the finest over bowled in a couple of generations of Test cricket, bowled against the run of the play and the luck of the weather and the toss; a sheer concentration of intelligence and courage and skill that swept away, in far less time that it has taken to write about it, three of the best batsmen who have ever played for England.

From *Sing all a green willow* by Ronald Mason, published by Epworth.

Colin Cowdrey

HAMBLEDON INTERLUDE

Colin Cowdrey was cricket Captain of Oxford, Kent and England. He scored twenty-seven Test centuries, and was awarded the C.B.E. for services to sport.

He has taken a great interest in the history and development of the game, and here he revives memories of the early Hambledon cricket.

HAMBLEDON INTERLUDE

I have just scored my first run at Hambledon, and taken a wicket too. It was a low-scoring match with the bowlers in command, just as it used to be 200 years ago.

The occasion was rather special. MCC, named aptly for this day "All England", were invited to send the best cricketers in the land to play against Hambledon to celebrate the bicentenary of cricket on Broadhalfpenny Down. Sadly, fixtures clashed. Someone had arranged a Test match against a visiting Australian XI at Nottingham. Again, a tobacco company had sponsored a County Cricket programme of matches called the John Player League. This sort of irreverence would have been frowned upon in the day that Richard Nyren owned the Bat and Ball Inn, but it would not have stopped the cricket. It did not deter this year's President, W.H. Webster, either, good player himself and an even finer Corinthian footballer. He accepted the challenge and instructed his two MCC secretaries to muster and lead some good men and true, worthy of the name of All England.

Without a member of the Nyren family still resident in the Bat and Ball, refreshment was taken in the lovely garden of local squire Charles Lutyens. His family, seeing our plight after the journey, showered hospitality upon us, so much so

Cricket

that it required a real effort to brace ourselves for the fierce afternoon encounter. We joined the huge concourse that was making its way to Broadhalfpenny Down where, with the weather good, the crowds had been gathering throughout the morning.

I doubt whether the ground has altered over the 200 years. The sight screens are new, of course, and there is a third stump in modern cricket with two bails. The bowling is no longer confined to under-arm as it was then. The Men of Hambledon would have been horrified to see us wearing pads, and I expect that they would have thought our modern equipment not a patch on that so beautifully manicured by John Small. I expected that the Hambledon captain would toss the bat for innings, thereby eliciting Jack Bailey's call of flat or round, but he did the next best thing. He flung up a golden guinea minted in 1777. Out captain won the toss, and a few minutes later we were batting for survival.

Weathering the storm
C.B. Fry's grandson, Charles, especially selected for his long experience of cricket in these parts, was brilliantly taken at slip, a great blow to All England. A.R. Day and I weathered the storm unconvincingly. I was conscious there was less betting around the ground than once there was, but there was quite a stir when my off-stump was removed. Fast bowlers Alan Mason and Danny Stephenson enjoyed the conditions, while Christopher Bazalgette in support floated the ball on to a sixpence. Robert Turner produced every sort of wile and spun the ball sharply. Somehow we notched 154 by tea, which was to prove a formidable total against our array of bowlers.

Hambledon sensed that they had a lot to do, but fought with enormous courage and a skill worthy of their forebears. Robert Turner played one of the memorable innings of modern cricket and just could have turned the match. With his team showing signs of panic in the field, John Bailey called for the ball and most unselfishly elected to bowl up the slope. There followed a tense piece of cricket, some magnificent fielding in the deep from Brian Hamblin and Michael Mence, Ted Clark quicksilver at short leg and M.G. Griffith keeping the wicket in brilliant fashion. Turner addressed himself to the task of over-throwing the menace of Bailey and produced some thunderous lofted blows to the deep field before he fell to an unplayable ball for 56. With no thought of a draw the Hambledon captain, Colin Barrett, hit three towering sixes in a last throw for victory while wickets fell at the other end. When the umpires came to draw stumps at the appointed hour eight wickets had fallen and Hambledon were just 30 runs short. The large crowd drifted away, proud that their village side had held the might of All England.

For me, it was a cricket experience that I would not have missed for the world. While I had come to accept that cricket had its first beginnings along the Weald, through Kent and Sussex, I have never visited Hambledon before nor fully appreciated its significance.

One thing puzzles me. How was it that this small village, miles from anywhere, suddenly became so precious to cricket and then, just as abruptly, lost its influence? For almost three decades the chief patrons and the best cricketers came to Hambledon and vast crowds found their way across the Downs to watch them. The Hambledon Club was formed soon after 1750 and yet by 1790 its power had declined and the focus of the game had moved to Thomas Lord's ground in Marylebone.

Today, Hambledon Cricket Club have their own ground in the village. The historic field at Broadhalfpenny Down forms part of the Winchester College estate and cricket is played there under the aegis of the Royal Navy at *HMS MERCURY*. The Bat and Ball Inn still nestles on the top corner of the ground and keeps watch, while on the field itself a lone stone monument stands to remind us of the Hambledon era.

From *Country Life*, 18 August 1977.

Michael Parkinson

WEBB

Michael Parkinson has earned international fame as a T.V. personality and interviewing compere. In addition, he has written humorous essays on soccer and cricket for the *Sunday Times*. The following one has a more serious note, and is a model of its kind.

WEBB

When I was five years old, the old man bought me a cricket bat. The blade was creamy, the handle red, and it was the best bat I ever possessed.

I picked it up for the first time and stood in the approved position, left shoulder pointing down the wicket, left toe cocked in honour of George Roberts, the local big hitter, who at the time I considered the best batsman in the world. My old man patiently took the bat from me, turned me so my right shoulder pointed down the wicket and nodded in satisfaction. Thus, a left-handed bat was created against nature's whims.

I didn't question the move at the time, but later the old man explained everything. 'No bowler likes left-handers lad. Remember that and think on that you've got a head start.' As a bowler himself he reckoned he knew what he was talking about. He hated bowling at 'caggy handers.'

When he finished bowling and became captain of our second team he worked on the simple philosophy that the more left-handed batsmen he could discover or invent the better our chances of victory. He proved his point by winning the championship with a team which included nine left-handed bats, four natural, five manufactured. He took great delight

Cricket

in the freakish nature of his team and loved observing the mounting incredulity of his opponents as left-handed bat followed left-handed bat to the wicket. After the first half dozen, the opposing captain would often turn to the old man, lurking on the boundary edge, and say, 'Ayup skipper. 'Ow many more bloody caggy 'anders siree?'

Whenever I think about that team I always begin wondering about the number of people who affect our outlook and attitudes on sport. I am cricket mad because I caught the complaint from my old man, but even that condition might have been cured had it not been for someone else. He was the sports master at the local grammar school, a large craggy man who had been good enough to play both football and cricket at professional level.

The first time I came across him he was bowling at the nets at we youngsters who were hoping to make the under-14 team. His first ball to me was a little short of a length and being young and full of madness I went for a hook and missed by a mile. It didn't seem very important to me and I was therefore a little taken aback on returning the ball to see the master, hands on hips, staring at the sky. He remained like that for some time, lips moving silently, and then he looked at me.

'What was that?' he asked.

'A hook sir,' I said. 'Hook?' he said shaking his head. 'A hook? At your age you shouldn't even know what it means.'

It was the best possible introduction to the man who for the next four years was to coach me in the game. He taught in the great Yorkshire tradition, concentrating solely on backward and forward defensive play. Any strokes we played that required the bat moving from the perpendicular were better done when he wasn't looking. I once played a late cut for four in a school game when I thought he was in bed with 'flu and as my eyes proudly followed the ball to the boundary, I saw him standing there sadly shaking his head at the horror of it all.

I once heard him admonish another master whom he caught demonstrating the square cut to a young player: 'Be it on your own head.'

For all he was a puritan about cricket he was a marvellous coach. He turned out a succession of young cricketers who were so well versed in the rudiments of the game that they found the transition from schoolboy cricket to the leagues fairly painless.

His one blind spot was a total inability to appreciate the

Cricket

odd exceptional talent that came his way. Everyone had to conform to his basic principles no matter how rich their natural gifts. At the time I was at school we had in our team a batsman called Hector of remarkable ability.

Hector, who was shaped like a junior Colin Milburn, had no time for acquiring defensive techniques. He approached each ball as if it was the last he would ever receive on this earth, and that being the case, he was going to try to split it in two. For a schoolboy he was an exceptional striker of the ball, blessed with a powerful physique, a quick eye and a sure sense of timing. He played some fine innings for the school teams, but no matter how brilliantly he played, he never pleased the sports master.

'Defence, Hector lad, defence,' the sports master would say, and Hector would put one foot down the track and blast the ball straight for six and the sports master would look sorrowful. The high point of their relationship occurred in a masters versus boys game in which the sports master opened the bowling and Hector opened the batting. He played one of his best innings that day, thrashing the bowling, particularly the sports master's, without mercy.

The master kept the ball up as he always taught us to do, and Hector kept thumping away. He had scored about 86 in 30 minutes when he hit over one of the sports master's deliveries and was bowled. As he walked towards the pavilion the sports master said triumphantly: 'I warned you Hector lad, that's what fancy play gets you.'

He was the only man on the field, or off it, who remained convinced that Hector had failed. It would have pleased him more if Hector had observed the rules that bound us lesser players and carried his bat for a dour thirty.

But for all that, he was a good man who taught a lot of boys a proper respect for the most difficult and beautiful of games.

When I saw him last, he looked old and ill and said he had retired as a sports master. He told me he watched the school team occasionally but had invariably been disappointed by what he saw. 'Too much flashing about, not enough straight bat,' he said.

He stood up to demonstrate his point. 'Cricket is about this . . .' He played forward with an imaginary bat. 'And this . . . ' He played back. 'And not this . . . ' And he executed what I can only describe as a derogatory late cut.

His name was Webb Swift and I heard recently that he had died. The chances are you've never heard of him. He wasn't

Cricket

a famous man, just important to a lot of people like me who learnt to love cricket at his knee, and whenever I think about people who have affected my life, I remember him.

From *Cricket Mad* by Michael Parkinson, published by Stanley Paul Ltd.

Ian Peebles

WOOLLEY: THE PRIDE OF KENT

Ian Peebles was one of the great cricketers whose playing experience has enriched their journalism.

He played for Middlesex and England in 1930 and against New Zealand in 1931.

He showed great ability in describing the humorous and unusual in cricketing scenes.

The following extract is from a chapter entitled "The Supreme Artist" in the book *Woolley: The Pride of Kent*.

From WOOLLEY: THE PRIDE OF KENT

It is naturally rather easier to acclaim the performance than to convey even a dim impression of it. Each innings was an event. There was always something almost dramatic about the appearance of this majestic figure. He walked unhurriedly but purposefully to the wicket amidst a buzz of anticipation on the part of the crowd and a well-founded apprehension on the part of most bowlers. On arrival at the crease there were no affectations or mannerisms, either of which would have been wholly alien to the scene. He would be given guard, glance down at the setting of the field and take stance. He stood upright, bending only so far as his height compelled him, feet slightly apart, hands high on the bat, the general effect being one of the ease and simplicity which characterised the whole performance.

There was about him an air of detachment, so that occasionally one got the impression that he was a casual, almost careless, starter. This was obviously not so, but I would say that, always eager to attack, it took him an over or two to get the feel of things and become warmed up. It might be added that this impression of indifference could be somewhat

Cricket

disconcerting to the opposition, acutely conscious that if they did not succeed immediately awful retribution was liable to befall them.

As the bowler reached the crease he would pick the bat up in a long, smooth circular sweep, parting his feet with a short, forward step of the right foot. The bat came down straight and firmly controlled close to the line of the off stump. There was plenty of time to make the choice of stroke and whatever it might be it was never otherwise than a flowing, rounded gesture. Never did one see a hasty stab or unbalanced jerk. His defence, being based chiefly on attack, did not have the rock-like impregnability of his contemporary, Philip Mead, but it was enormously aided by the fact that he was a most difficult man to bowl at. Once he was going there was no area in which the bowler could seek shelter. He had all the strokes, and he lent to them an unequalled force and beauty. Thus, when one is asked what was his best shot, it is impossible to say, for whatever he did was enthralling. He was a beautiful off-side player off back and front foot, driving, cutting, slicing to all sectors. I have frequently quoted what I consider to be the prettiest compliment ever paid on the field of cricket. It was at Canterbury in 1930 that Frank took 60 undefeated off the Australians in double-quick time. The first burst came chiefly off Alan Fairfax, a very high-class quick-medium bowler, who was lathered against all sections of the off-side fence. Seeking reassurance, he asked that fine rumbustious character Vic Richardson if he thought it was 'all right bowling at his off stump'. 'All right,' said Vic enthusiastically, 'it's bloody marvellous—we're all enjoying it.'

Frank was the most exhilarating straight hitter. The action seldom appeared to be more than a free-swinging forward stroke, but the ball would sail away to clear the longest boundary. He loved to treat fast bowlers so and when in frustration they dropped the ball short he would pull them square with the same unhurried venom. This was essentially a pull, made with the full long-armed swing of the bat as the striker lay back on his left leg. The hook was somehow too angular a movement ever to fit into this flowing repertoire.

It was a dominating as well as a graceful performance, the batsman sailing serenely on his chosen course in all circumstances, disrupting and ignoring opposing stratagems.

At Tonbridge, when Walter Robins and myself were young and cock-a-hoop at getting a couple of early wickets, Pat Hendren indicated Frank's dominating figure advancing on the scene. 'Here comes the lion-tamer,' said he. It proved an apt description and when we had been flogged out of sight Nigel Haig devised a somewhat desperate device. Harry Lee, at square-leg, was to keep dropping back until he was right on the boundary, and Nigel would then bowl the fifth ball of the over short. To a point the plan worked out. Nigel dropped the ball short and Frank slapped it away straight in the desired direction. However, it bisected the line of the fielder's upturned eyes about eight feet above his head and went 'thwup' into a tent behind, so that the structure tugged at its moorings and shimmered like a belly-dancer. All, especially the fielder, were rather relieved that the plan had not worked out in the final detail.

He *hit* the ball beautifully on the leg side with the same full rhythmical swing of the bat. One stroke particularly pleases the memory and seems to be a penchant of left-handers, as Graeme Pollock also plays it to perfection. It is the pull-drive played off the front foot to the good-length or overpitched ball in the region of the leg stump. Ideally, this is played to the faster bowling, when the rise of the ball aids the 'take-off' and it goes sweet and far between mid-wicket and long-on.

. . . . . .

Frank never expressed any preference for, nor prejudice against, any particular type of bowling. One would surmise that he enjoyed himself to the utmost against the fast bowlers. It was against them that he produced his most startling effects, and it was inspiring and amusing to see him quell any ill-advised attempts at retaliation. He was not a man to be intimidated and, not unnaturally, he had a fine confidence in his own powers of counter-attack. If he was hit he considered that he was the party to blame, and he was never heard to complain or speak a rancorous word against anyone who bowled aggressively. Indeed, he had little reason to do so, for the bouncer was ever grist to his mill.

He considered McDonald and Larwood the fastest bowlers he had ever played, and thought the latter the fairest and best. To watch him opposed to either must have been to see the highest expression of the game of cricket. I never myself saw him tackle McDonald but I played in a North *v.* South Trial match at Old Trafford where he opened the innings against Larwood and Voce at full blast. He got 50 out of 72

Cricket

in less than an hour. Always having a slight flair for the anticlimax, he lathered this powerful combination into retirement with joy and ease, and was then caught at long-on off a full-toss from Tommy Mitchell.

From *Woolley: The Pride of Kent* by Ian Peebles, published by The Cricketer Ltd and Hutchinson & Co Ltd.

Alan Gibson

A BATTING MACHINE THEY CALLED `THE CROUCHER´

Alan Gibson wrote on cricket and rugby in the *Times* and the *Sunday Times*. He was a B.B.C. commentator for Test Matches and Rugby internationals. He also made a considerable reputation as a versatile broadcaster on many well-known programmes. His sketches of famous sporting personalities are beautifully, and often wittily, drawn.

A BATTING MACHINE THEY CALLED 'THE CROUCHER'

> "At one end stocky Jessop
>   frowns,
> The human catapult
> Who wrecks the roofs of
>   distant towns
> When set in his assault"

So wrote an American rhymester in 1897, when G.L. Jessop, a young man scarcely over the threshold of his career, was playing in Philadelphia. "The human catapult" was a fine hyperbole. The way Jessop sprang at the ball, the moment the bowler had released it, is what those who saw him most vividly remember.

English cricket has had bigger hitters than Jessop (he did not try for specially long hits: the boundary was good enough). English cricket has had batsmen who scored more runs with a higher average. But there has never been an English batsman who hit so hard, and scored so fast, and yet still scored runs so consistently. In his career, which lasted from 1894 to 1914, Jessop scored 26,698 runs, at an average of 32.63, and if one believes all one hears—those in Gloucestershire who remember him never tire of talking about him—hardly played a defensive stroke.

Shortly before Roy Webber died, he was talking to me about some statistical investigations he had been making into Jessop's career. Jessop scored 53 centuries in first-class cricket, with a highest score of 286, and so far as Roy had been able to discover, he had never batted for more than three hours. I don't know if Roy had time to confirm this, but it is an astonishing thought. Take into account your different social climate, your changed over rate, your negative bowling tactics: take into account anything you like, but to score all those runs and all those centuries, and not to bat for more than three hours. . . .

In his early days Jessop was a successful fast bowler, twice taking 100 wickets in a season; and throughout his career he had a reputation for being one of the world's best covers fieldsmen. A.C. MacLaren, recalled to the England captaincy in 1909, demanded before the series began that Jessop should be picked for every Test, "because he will run Victor Trumper out for me". This plan did not work—rather the contrary, for Jessop strained his back while fielding in the third Test, and never played for England again—but it is a remarkable example of the value placed upon his fielding.

I felt I glimpsed a little of G.L. Jessop once, when I saw his son, the Rev. G.L.O. Jessop, score a fast 80 or so for Dorset against Cornwall at Camborne. G.L.O. Jessop was then middle-aged himself, but a beautiful striker of the ball. He used the sweep a lot, as his father is said to have done, sometimes in the most daring circumstances, but he also had a splendid straight drive back over the bowler's head.

C.B. Fry always insisted that Jessop was not "a slogger", which used to be a pejorative term, but a true batsman who took risks, who stretched his technique to the limit, sometimes attempting more than he could achieve; but was nevertheless basically a sound player. That innings by G.L.O. Jessop, though he has never sought to compare his merits with those of his father, gave me a fairly clear idea of what Fry meant.

In Test cricket, it must be said, Jessop's record was disappointing. Although he was usually picked when he was available, over a period of ten years, he scored only 569 runs in 18 matches, at an average of 21.88.

Nevertheless, Jessop did win a Test, the famous one against Australia in 1902, when he redeemed a forlorn English cause in the last innings, scoring 104, his only Test century, in 75 minutes. The philosophy behind picking him must always have been "Ah! But whatever his average, he's the kind of man who can swing a match", and that was an occasion when he did.

The number of times he did it for other sides, and particularly Gloucestershire, it would be a labour to count. He came to the Gloucestershire captaincy soon after the departure of W.G. Grace. Grace had left amid a large and loud rumpus, and Jessop's task was not an easy one. But although he was unable to lead the side to the championship, which was hardly surprising with the resources at his disposal, he kept up the gates and the spirit of Gloucestershire as much by his own marvellous example as anything else, and today his name is spoken of in the county in the same breath as those of Grace and of Hammond.

He was nicknamed "The Croucher". He bent low at the wicket, and sometimes would stoop down so far that his cap was on the level of the bails. He said that this helped him to judge the length of a ball early. It must have added considerably to the psychological and dramatic effects of his sudden spring, his pounce, his leap at the ball. But in later life, at least, he disliked the name.

About 1948, when I was a junior producer on the staff of the BBC, I was sent a capital script about Jessop, by Harold Gardiner, called "The Croucher". We put the programme into production, and billed it in the *Radio Times*. As a matter of courtesy, we sent a script to Jessop, though, as it was an almost entirely laudatory script, we hardly thought he would complain. But he did. He complained most sharply, particularly about the title: indeed, it took all the tact of Frank Gillard to calm him down, and the programme was postponed, to be broadcast at a later date under the less inflammatory title of "G.L. Jessop".

Well, most old men have cantankerous moments, but this incident has always baffled me. Did he resent the nickname because it was put upon him by the press? He did a good deal of journalism himself at one time and another. Did he resent it because the Gloucestershire public relished it? Amateurs in those days were inclined to disregard public esteem, but he must have been proud of the affection in which Gloucestershire held him (he was born and brought up at Cheltenham), and it is as "The Croucher"—the great cat about to jump— that he is still happily and proudly remembered.

From the *Times*, 18 May 1974.

Geoffrey Moorhouse

THE ROSES MATCH

Geoffrey Moorhouse has been a prolific and successful writer whose works have included accounts of a 2,000-mile solo journey across the Sahara, and of his experiences as a trawlerman in the Grand Banks, Newfoundland.

In 1978, he spent this vital year, when Kerry Packer had thrown down the gauntlet to established cricket, in watching games at many levels throughout the country, and trying to assess the varied appeal of "The Best Loved Game". The range included a Test Match, the Village Championship, Eton v. Harrow, Lancashire League, the Gillette Cup Final, the Hambledon Game, and here The Roses Match.*

THE ROSES MATCH

May 27   *Headingley*
YORKSHIRE v LANCASHIRE

One approaches this day as others attend a Trooping of the Colour or a Last Night of the Proms, with a sense of occasion that only participants in a mythology can feel. I was brought up on three legends that combined to keep the family's blood astir, when it might otherwise have grown sluggish with the passing of the years. One was the Lancashire Landing at Gallipoli, where Grandad actually played. Another was the victory of the Wanderers (Bolton's, you understand) at the first Wembley Final, where Dad claims he was fouled by the policeman's white horse. The third was the Roses Match. Not any particular game between Lancs and Yorks,

---

*Two matches are played in a year, home and away, between Lancashire and Yorkshire (counties of the Red and White Rose).

mind; just the Roses Match. This was different from the other two because it was a legend still being made and, by apostolic succession, its future was still partly in our hands. It was of sacramental significance in our calendar, like Whit Walks and Wakes Week, and even if none of us actually got down to Old Trafford or over the hill to Headingley or Bramall Lane, we never went anywhere else while the game was on. Gardening was the order of the day then, with the living room radio going full blast, and Dad sucking his teeth at the tomato plants whenever Washbrook played and missed. Migration to the south in pursuit of trade put a stop to much of my own attendance at the rite, but it dogs me still, as much as any of Francis Thompson's ghosts. When I manage to get up for the Roses Match, I remember who I am and what it is that I am about: not just a spectator at a cricket match this time, but a man with a responsibility to discharge, so that a legend shall live on into the recollection of his children. It is almost the only event which I allow to justify the wearing of a tie, for it is unthinkable that I should turn up (in the enemy camp most of all) without that dark blue silk sprinkled with the neat red roses of my county.

My handicap is that I have always found it hard to whip up the proper degree of belligerence towards the Yorkshire team; much less towards the Yorkshire crowd. There is none more knowledgeable about the game, or fairer in its judgment of skilful play by a cricketer of whichever side. And here, even more than at Old Trafford I think, the spectators themselves are liable to make any cricket match a memorable one. I remember Headingley in the 1961 Test against Benaud's side, when May and Cowdrey were making very heavy weather of the Australian attack. They were together for an age, scoring only a handful of runs, and I think that (when May was out) it must have been the only time an English captain's dismissal was greeted with cheers by Englishmen, so grateful were we that part of our boredom was done. In came Ted Dexter, the young lion of that year, who at once began to call for sharp singles, which had been neglected for far too long. Cowdrey's bulky figure responded gallantly to each call, but they were clearly costing him a lot of puff. After one mighty charge to the other end, in which he only just made his ground, he overran the crease by yards and stood panting in some distress. A "Hey" of relief went round Headingley as the runout was forestalled. As this died down, a voice pickled in the West Riding boomed out from somewhere near my bench. "Now steady on, Dexter. Yer'll 'ave Cowdrey thin

Cricket

as a bloody rake bi close o' play if yer go on like this!" Professional gag men are paid quite a lot of money for lines like that.

That was on such a day as this one, with a hot sun burning from a cloudless morning sky. After the wettest spring I can remember in a long time, with matches rained off all over the land, the weather has turned perfect for our pilgrimage to Leeds. Girls striding towards the match through the trenchwork of bricked terraces off the Otley Road, have abandoned tights in favour of bare legs. Long before the players appear, the caravan by the grandstand is doing brisk business in white sunhats with the Yorkshire colours in a band above the brim; by lunchtime the Headingley crowd will look like a convention from the smarter bowling greens of the south, taking a day off to watch this alien game in the north. But those hats represent commitment as much as protection from the sun, and the hundreds wearing them roar their encouragement when Hampshire leads his team down the dressing room stairs and the players come bounding out on to the turf. Boycott is nursing a sore thumb and Old is out with a bruised foot, absences which must tilt the scales heavily Lancashire's way, but I do not hear anyone around me complaining at this ill-luck. As Wood and David Lloyd come out to bat, Headingley seems to be preparing itself spiritually for a long day of siege, willing its troops to stick to their task without the anointed chief and his most potent aide. I have no doubt, myself, that Hayes was wise in deciding to bat first. After two or three days of this drying heat, that pitch should be good for plenty of runs. No one on the ground can have an inkling of the sensations to come.

From *The Best Loved Game* by Geoffrey Moorhouse, published by Hodder & Stoughton Ltd. Reprinted by permission of Hodder & Stoughton Ltd.

Soccer

J.L. Carr

HOW STEEPLE SINDERBY WANDERERS WON THE F.A. CUP

J.L. Carr in *How Steeple Sinderby Wanderers Won the F.A. Cup* takes the archetypal David v. Goliath theme and gives as its climax a successful confrontation for Steeple Sinderby Wanderers against the Rangers in the final of the F.A. Cup. The novel is written in the form of a rough draft for a future Official History, and some of the story is told through newspaper reports and radio broadcasts. At the beginning of the extract is a newspaper report of the quarter-final against Manchester. The amusing story gains added impact from its rural setting and characters.

J.L. Carr also wrote a cricket novel (*A Season in Sinji*) and *The Harpole Report*.

From HOW STEEPLE SINDERBY WANDERERS WON THE F.A. CUP

STAGGERING THAT'S SINDERBY

In a match of rare excitement Steeple Sinderby Wanderers, the side from the back end of Nowhere, rose at the final fences like a thoroughbred giving the tiny privileged crowd glimpse upon glimpse of the flush of true greatness. It was performance enough to daunt whichever of the three sides the draw will reveal as their opponents in the Semi-Final of the F.A. Cup. Nothing in Manchester's experience possibly could have prepared them for the ordeal which they endured, and nothing could have armoured them against the swift and deadly flow of football that engulfed them. At the end of the day, when all was done, they were well content to leave with self-respect. There was nothing for them, or for that matter, any other club, on this parish midden, except dusty defeat.

Soccer

But there was a time when sheer professionalism came into its own and Manchester dominated the game, but then it was seventy-two minutes too late and Sinderby's determination was not to be cracked. They gritted their teeth and, somehow, held on.

The drive and confidence of the home side's opening assault forced Manchester defenders deeper upon each other. And still the villagers found spaces for Montague, Slangsby and Sledmore to plot, spaces for Wimslow and Montague to run and that single fatal space for the Shooting Star himself to turn and blast the only goal of the match. Yet in the brilliant dawn-of-the-game, Slangsby hit the bar, Montague an upright and, on two occasions, the ball wobbled dangerously along the goal line before Goddard put it clear.

Manchester played to a level of defence no team could have bettered. Assault after assault was repulsed and the two runs by Butlin and a superb flick by Dyson were mere gestures by their own forwards. They could not break out of their own half long enough to sustain a raid to deserve the name of reprisal.

Even so, it was not until the dying quarter that the home side scored, a muddled effort undeserving of the context of so fine a game. From a free kick Slangsby came in fast to have his shot blocked, the sprawling Goddard managing to turn it out to Jennings who, never having known the great Swift in the days of his glory, dawdled a stride too long. Dispossession and shot were almost one movement. The ball struck the inner angle of upright and crossbar and crashed into a corner of the net.

From that moment Sinderby faced counter attacks of such ferocity that, until yesterday, I would have supposed no side could have survived . . .

And yet this Homeric struggle took place in almost Sabbath calm, witnessed by a mere 1,800 privileged people. But, outside the Plow, it is said more than 20,000 fans were sustained by local reporter, Alice Trigger's tattered tale of the game . . .

All true: he can't be faulted. And yet it was not all. He saw only the game. And the major drama had moved beyond it, for, as the church clock reminded them that only ten minutes were left and still no equalizing goal, foreboding of disaster spread through orchard and paddock and street black with people. And a strange and awe-inspiring sound rose — a vast meaningless roar that went on and on. Not the usual match noise that surges and sinks, but an animal roar like some primeval creature wounded to the death and questioning its fate. It alarmed me. And not just me, our players began to be jittery. Giles Montagu told me later that he felt that they were being willed to lose, that this great blind multitude would tear them apart in an agony of frustration and destroy, not only them, but the village and, last, themselves.

We were being dragged down by sheer noise.

Soccer

Then ...... THEN!

Then Mr. Fangfoss, in his office of churchwarden, rose to yet more glorious stature. Pondering what he had been told about noise and crowds, he had called out the ringers on standby and put their duty to them. And, at a sign from him, and not a moment too soon, the bells burst into the great Grandsire Triple, which had never been attempted in our belfry since Queen Victoria's Jubilee. It was indeed a Great and Mighty Wonder and such a din quelling all other din can never have been heard before on any football ground, crashing and reeling down upon the village, stunning player and concourse alike.

And, in this truly appalling uproar, the game ended. Though no more than two or three players heard the whistle go. The news just spread as it was seen that some no longer bothered to pursue the ball. Then the bells decelerated and stopped and the crowd stumbled dizzily away in a silence that seemed louder than sound.

From *How Steeple Sinderby Wanderers Won the F.A. Cup*, by J.L. Carr, published by London Magazine Editions.

Brian Glanville
WORLD CUP FINAL, '66

Brian Glanville has been Soccer Correspondent on the *Sunday Times* since 1958, seeing British football in its global context. He is also a novelist and short-story writer. He gives one of the best accounts of England's success in the World Cup in 1966.

WORLD CUP FINAL, '66

England's was a glorious team performance, yet one must still pick out a star, and that star is Alan Ball. Seldom can the little, red-haired Blackpool player have shown such inexhaustible stamina. Never, certainly, has he shown such exhilarating skill, such elegant control and footwork, such devastating use of the ball. This, too, against a full-back of world class like Schnellinger, one who has subdued in his time the finest in the game. In this exhibition, however, Ball himself is among the finest in the game, and no back could have subdued him today.

The all-round excellence of his play overshadowed even Bobby Charlton's but Charlton played, once more, with the greatest fluency and the most impressive technique. Peters was a splendid ally to him in midfield—a goal scorer, too—while Hurst's ability in the air was a weapon without which victory could never have been won. This, though it was with his right foot that he scored England's third goal, his left foot that he scored the fourth.

One would write more happily about Germany's performance had it not been for the displeasing nature of their equalising goal. But they are a team which deserves appreciation, a team about which there's an impressive aura of controlled power and technical aplomb. Athletic, incisive, and intelligent, they were scarcely recognisable from the weary side one had seen at Goodison last Monday.

Beckenbauer not only shouldered the burden of looking after Charlton but worked with poise and sophistication in midfield throughout the match. Held's powerful, courageous running, down the left, was a menace almost to the end; Seeler showed similar pertinacity and courage. Had Emmerich only matched them in ability and determination, the result might have been different.

Germany's tactics, like England's, were fluid. Schulz "swept up" behind a line of four backs which intermittently included Beckenbauer. When Beckenbauer broke, he linked with the gifted but variable Overath. Slightly in front of these, something rather short of a spearhead, played Haller, while ahead of him, again, there was a treble threat of Seeler, Held and Emmerich.

Seeler in the first half, looked for space on the empty right flank—where Haller figured for much of the second. Held, as one has remarked, frequently found it on the left.

In the tense, mutually exploratory first stages of the game, it was Schulz whom one noticed more than anybody, playing with fine anticipation and calm, moving to and fro across the penalty box like a faithful bird dog, fetching and retrieving, impeccably finding his man.

It was after eight minutes of this nervous football on a difficult, wet ground, that England made the first attack of any consequence. Hunt's crossfield ball to Stiles was admirable; so was the centre which followed. Tilkowski went up to it with a fellow defender, neither got it, and Bobby Charlton put it accurately back again. This time, Hurst soared up with Tilkowski, who pushed the ball uneasily away, to finish flat on the ground requiring treatment. One recalled that after last Monday, his injured shoulder had made him doubtful for the game.

Scarcely was he up on his feet than England were testing him again. Jackie Charlton, breaking purposefully upfield, squared the ball to Peters. The half-back, from some thirty yards, shot hard along the ground. Tilkowski got to it with a flailing of arms, pushing the ball round the post.

But with thirteen minutes gone, a mistake utterly untypical of the English defence gave Germany the lead. Wilson, going up to a cross from the left, met it well enough, only to head it straight down to the feet of Haller. The blond inside-forward

Soccer

thankfully accepted the gift, killing the ball, then shooting low across Banks into the far corner of the goal.

The prospect was ominous; one of Germany shutting up shop and taking the World Cup with that goal. The noise from the terraces was that of a small Nuremberg Rally.

But within six minutes, England, surprisingly, were level. Overath, who had just been penalised for tripping Ball, now tripped Moore, and paid a heavy forfeit.

Moore was up in a trice, to swing his free kick across the goal. Hurst, his West Ham colleague, came rushing to it from the opposite side, through a surprised German defence, to head perfectly and powerfully into the left-hand corner. The gestures of Germany's defenders must surely have been those of astonishment as much as protest. The game was open again.

Free kicks were abundant. Peters gave one away, had his name taken by the referee, and when Schnellinger took the kick Seeler got up to it with some of his old spring. Though he out-jumped the English defence, however, his header ended safely in Banks's arms.

But Seeler was as good, throughout the first half, on the ground as in the air. Taking a pass from Beckenbauer he twisted round Moore, and put through Haller, but Banks had time to take the ball in comfort.

It had settled down to be an intelligent, delicately balanced, technically adroit game, each side building up neatly in midfield, England dangerous not only thanks to the fluent authority of Bobby Charlton, but thanks also to the vulnerability of Tilkowski, in the German goal.

Thus, after thirty-four minutes, a move begun by Wilson, carried on by Hunt, Stiles and Bobby Charlton, ended with a cross by Cohen, a header by Hurst. It was hardly more than a touch, but Tilkowski weakly pushed the ball out. Before he could retrieve it, lively little Ball had whipped it away from him across the goal but the ball was narrowly cleared.

Three minutes more, and Germany—twice—came even closer. Held, boring in forcefully along the left wing, was stopped with equal force by Jackie Charlton. Held took the corner himself, and the ball was indecisively headed out, reaching an unmarked Overath. The inside-left, familiar with Wembley since schoolboy days, shot coolly and strongly. Banks blocked it, could not hold it, and Emmerich shot again. He was considerably closer in, but this time Banks safely held the ball.

After forty-two minutes, Hurst's formidable ability in the

air should have given England their second. Rising to Wilson's cross, he nodded the ball precisely to Hunt, on his left. Not for the first time, the German defence stood curiously entranced—but it was Hunt they had to deal with, not Greaves; an honest player who hooked an honest left-foot shot. Tilkowski raised his arms, possibly in prayer, and blocked it.

Within the minute the inextinguishable Seeler's right-foot shot had forced Banks into a difficult tip over the bar.

It had been beyond question a first half of pleasing quality but unexpected error, quite free from the negativity that we had feared.

The second half began with a heavy shower, and two fine intricate pieces of control by Ball, setting free first Cohen, then Stiles. Ball had already been one of the heroes of the first half, moving across the breadth of the field with astonishing energy and industry, followed everywhere by Schnellinger, as though by some huge, blond German nanny.

After this, the game settled down to a protracted period of stalemate, in which its eventual high drama was scarcely implicit. Some of the pace and sharpness had gone, and if England's imposing defence now palpably had the measure of Germany's clever attack, England's forwards did not seem to have the skills to penetrate Germany's white wall. Their chief weapon continued to be the glorious leap, the skilled aerial deflections of Hurst, while Ball was as active, Bobby Charlton as graceful, as ever. On the ground, the English spearhead, Hunt especially, could make little progress. And if Peters was still coming through with judgement and élan, there was, inevitably, no threat coming from the empty left wing.

Not till eighteen minutes from the end did a goal seem seriously feasible. Then, from Peters's swinging centre, Hurst got up—yet again. Once more, he got the merest touch to the ball, but it was enough to guide it to Bobby Charlton, whose shot, flying across the face of the goal, curled tantalisingly outside the far post.

There were twelve and a half minutes left when England at last went into the lead. Ball, forcing a corner on the right, took it himself, and out of the goalmouth confusion the ball ran to Hurst. Hurst thumped it immediately, with more hope than certainty. But into the packed defence it went and there, wonder of wonders, spun off a German defender to sit up begging, in the goal mouth. Two red shirts rushed in for the kill; Peters it was who smashed the ball into goal.

After the hugging, the congratulations, Stiles and Wilson

turned desperately to the touchline, fingers upstretched, eyebrows quizzingly raised, asking how long there was to go.

With four minutes left, England, had they only kept their heads, must inevitably have scored again, putting the result beyond appeal. Ball's superb pass sent Hunt racing through on the left, Bobby Charlton and Hurst on his right, only Schulz between them and Tilkowski's goal. A three to one situation, in which simple accuracy must have brought a goal. But Hunt's pass was too shallow and too square, Charlton's shot a hastily hit fiasco.

In the very last minute, England paid heavily for their carelessness. Emmerich took a free kick of doubtful origin; Schnellinger, in the goalmouth, played the ball down blatantly and undeniably with his hand. While the English defence, the English supporters, looked on appalled, Weber hit the ball past Banks into the net, and Herr Dienst, incredibly, allowed a goal. No wonder poor Jackie Charlton sat on the ground, his head in his hands, the very picture of a man tried beyond endurance.

Extra time began, appropriately, with yet another run by the indestructible Ball, a fine run down the right, a fine shot, which might have given England back the lead, after ninety seconds. But Tilkowski tipped it bravely over the bar.

Then Jackie Charlton turned a ball back to his brother on the edge of the box, for an insidious left-foot shot which Tilkowski launched himself to turn splendidly, full stretch, on the right hand post.

Germany, too, however, had shots left in the locker. Held, leaving Ball and Jackie Charlton gasping, tore down the left wing for a cross which everybody, defender and attacker alike, missed.

Then, with one hundred minutes gone, justice was belatedly done; England scored again. Stiles's fine, long pass to the right put Ball totally clear. From somewhere or other, that remarkable little man, more sprite than footballer, found the energy for yet another burst. His centre on the run was perfectly executed. Hurst met it with a thundering right-foot shot which left Tilkowski helpless as a statue. The ball hit the under side of the bar and came down—surely over the line?

Yet after that iniquitous German goal, all was possible and we waited for interminable seconds, died a thousand deaths, while little Herr Dienst trotted over to his Russian linesman. The linesman gestured obscurely but dramatically—was he giving a goal, or indicating that the ball had bounced on the line? And then, at last, we saw Herr Dienst pointing to the middle. England, once more, were ahead.

Nor was it to be their final goal. In the very last seconds, as boys dashed ecstatic on to the field, Hurst ran on and on alone through a strange hiatus, a petrified, exhausted German defence, to shoot his third goal, England's fourth. The sun was shining now—shining for England.

From the *Sunday Times*, 31 July 1966, reprinted by courtesy of John Farquharson Ltd.

Hugh McIlvanney
THE BRAZILIANS

Hugh McIlvanney has had a distinguished career, having written widely on sports and world affairs. He has been one of the leaders of the *Observer* team of reporters covering recent World Cups, and writes here an assessment of Brazil's players in their World Cup team of 1970 in Mexico.

He has a dynamic, emphatic style of writing.

THE BRAZILIANS

Brazil were now stirred to put on the style. After a penetrating exchange of passes between Gérson and Pelé, Gérson just failed to pull the ball clear of the last tackle. When Pelé passed to Tostão the centre-forward did move into the open, drifting beautifully to his left, but his crisp shot was touched over the bar by Viktor. Next Pelé, gloriously ubiquitous, came out of a challenge with the ball and raced fifty yards. Tostão and Jairzinho between them could not quite exploit the chance he made.

Undismayed, Pelé brought the first half to an amazing climax with one of the great moments of the World Cup. Moving into possession well inside his own half of the field, he gave a barely perceptible glance in the direction of Viktor, saw that the goalkeeper had moved out some yards from the posts, and struck. Pelé was still in the Brazilian segment of the centre circle when, raising his right leg in a prodigious backlift and swinging it through with a flowing, effortless precision worthy of an iron shot by Ben Hogan, he sent the ball in a fast arc towards goal. Viktor's contorted features revealed the extent of his painful astonishment as he scrambled back under the ball, then spun helplessly to see it swoop less than a yard outside a post.

Through the interval the stadium throbbed with the special excitement crowds feel when they have seen something remarkable and know there is more of the same to come. Without question, Brazil appeared capable of the explosion Captain Coutinho had promised. Pelé *had* created his mood. He was playing as many Europeans had never seen him play before. Some, forgivably misled by seeing him in his low phases when he was drained from over-use, had come to suspect that his was an inflated legend. Now they were savouring the correction. As early as this point, we could see that Pelé's statement that he was fitter than he had been for half-a-dozen years was no mere Press release. He looked marvellous, like a hungry animal that was quick and strong enough to kill but too wise in the chase to start running prematurely. In addition to all his gifts — the almost supernatural athleticism, the force and subtlety and completeness of his play, the capacity for making deeply considered moves as if they were spontaneous — in addition to all this, there was an unfailing sense of relevance in everything he did. Concentration enclosed him like an extra skin. He was in almost all important respects the most experienced World Cup player in the competition and he knew exactly what mattered and what did not. He knew that to try with every fibre, which he was determined to do, he must stay relaxed, constantly rejecting any temptation to make the unprofitable flourish. Until the job was done, the roar of the crowd would sound far out on the borders of his mind.

Even playing like this, Pelé did not dwarf the men around him. Brazil's central asset, we could see already and indeed had realised before a ball was kicked, was the plurality of exceptional talents. Gérson, his encroaching baldness and fleshless face making him look older than twenty-nine, acted as an inspired supply officer behind the front line. His left foot (it is an accident if he uses his right) has the accuracy to drop the ball in a butterfly net from fifty yards and the power to knock down a goalpost. The other members of the team call him The Parrot because they have never known a parrot that talked as much. But they admit that he is worth listening to.

Alongside Gérson, although he often gave old-fashioned justification to the number eleven on his back by thrusting down the left wing, was Rivelino, a handsome son of Italian parents who would be a tremendous player even if his left foot did not shoot as hard as any in the world. Tostão, too, is essentially left-footed, which adds to his prestige among Brazilians. It is a matter of history that the most feared strikers of the ball in their game, the legendary thunderers, have been left-footed. Few of them have had the comprehensive skills of Tostão. He is a short man with a thick torso and immense legs that appear as big round the ankles as some players' are round the calf. There is a marked contrast with Pelé, who has massive slabs of muscle down to the knee, then tapers fine as a schoolgirl to his feet. Tostão has pleasant but rather blunt features under sparse dark hair that is curly in a wispy way. His eyes move slowly in his face, suggesting weariness with the familiarity of what they see, or hold a steady gaze as if looking through the turmoil around him to something in the far distance. There is an impression of maturity and quiet authority that makes it difficult to remember that he is only twenty-four years old. In this first match Tostão was straining to adjust. Playing far forward, often with his back to the goal, it was his responsibility to go where the concentration of defenders was thickest, so that he could employ his delicately judged one-touch manoeuvres to take opponents out of the game. At first his reactions were sluggish by his own standards but soon the barnacles accumulated by disuse were peeling away and by the end of the match there were clear signs that he would be a dominant influence on the competition.

Jairzinho had no real problems of fitness. The Negro winger admits a susceptibility to injury that surprised those who have marvelled at the great feline strength of a physique which would fit a top welterweight boxer. Part of the explanation is that following the 1966 World Cup he lost a year's action as a result of breaking the same bone in his right foot twice and only recovered after an operation had inserted a sliver of bone from elsewhere in his body. Despite this, in his determination to go through any barrier put in front of him, he exposes himself to maximum hazard. Zagalo wisely declined to pressure Jairhinzo when he showed poor form in practice. 'He gave me confidence to save myself for the match and it worked,' the forward said afterwards. Even in the match itself he conserved energy, keeping his most devastating runs for the second half. It was a pattern he would confirm in later performances. He grew stronger as others wilted, and the sight of him gathering speed for one of his surges at goal came to be a major terror of defenders' lives. With the ball kept close between his feet, but bobbing deceptively loose rather than running submissively, he went at his challengers as if he found their very presence an insufferable affront. Those he could not skirt cleanly he was happy to barge aside. In these collisions he constantly appeared on the point of losing his balance but hardly ever did. That was left to the defenders.

The Czechs had encountered problems from the outset in Guadalajara. The rough field allotted to them at a local school took such a toll on their ankles that they switched to an area attached to a brewery, an act of masochism in such thirsty weather. On their return to the school Horvath, the captain and roving interceptor in the defence, and Adamec promptly hurt themselves. At the interval in the Jalisco Stadium we wondered if Horvath and Adamec might not have been better off with injuries serious enough for them to be excused duties against Brazil. The second half, we felt, was not likely to be restful for them or for Viktor.

But the score was still 1-1 and Czechoslovakia, having substituted the elongated, shambling figure of Kvasnak for the short, hustling Hrdlicka, restarted with a show of defiance. Petras made ground on the right and passed to Frantisek Vesely, who might have responded with something better than two shots against Félix's body. Brazil's answer was vivid. Pelé from the right slipped the ball short to Gérson, outside the penalty area in front of goal. The shot, struck early with the left foot, bent viciously outwards and Viktor did not move as it thudded on to his right-hand post. Gérson claimed perfect compensation in the sixtieth minute. From the depths of the midfield he aimed a long diagonal pass high towards Pelé as the great forward edged round behind Hagara. The ball, having travelled all of fifty yards, looked to be curving within reach of Hagara's jump but Gérson's judgment was so fine that it narrowly cleared the left-back's head and dropped on to Pelé's chest as he made his own leap. Pelé chested it down in front of him and took an unhurried step forward before meeting it on the bounce with his right instep to place it in the far side-netting.

From *World Cup '70* edited by Hugh McIlvanney and Arthur Hopcraft, published by Eyre & Spottiswoode Ltd.

Arthur Hopcraft
EULOGY

Arthur Hopcraft (born in 1932) had a brilliant journalistic career with the *Guardian*, the *Observer*, the *Sunday Times*, and as a freelance. He was also a television playwright.

He wrote a book on the problems of hunger and poverty in the world. *The Football Man*, from which the following extract is taken, is a psychological and sociological investigation of what John Moynihan has called "The Soccer Syndrome".

His appraisal of Bobby Charlton gives an outstanding assessment of the charisma of the best loved of footballers.

EULOGY

Everyone who follows football has his favourite player; even the players do. The selection is bound to reflect something of the nature of the one who is doing the choosing. The favourite is not necessarily being named as the greatest player of all. We may admit, reluctantly, our favourite's weaknesses. What we are saying is that this particular player appeals to us more than any other. It has to do with his personality, his style of behaviour, perhaps importantly the way in which he compensates for his deficiencies. He is the player who may disappoint sometimes with a ragged, off-form performance, and yet over the years stays clear and bright in the memory. He is the player we bring to mind first when we ask ourselves what football looks like when we enjoy it most. The man I name for this role is Bobby Charlton.

The flowing line of Charlton's football has no disfiguring barbs in it, but there is a heavy and razor-sharp arrowhead at its end. It is the combination of the graceful and the dramatic which makes him so special. There are few players who affect a crowd's response as much as he does. Something extraordinary is expected of him the moment he receives the ball. He can silence a crowd instantly, make it hold its breath in expectation. A shot from Charlton, especially if hit on the run from outside the penalty area, is one of the great events of the sport, not because it is rare, which it is not, but because the power of it is massive and it erupts out of elegance; he is never clumsy or desperate in movement; he can rise very close to the athletic ideal.

The persistent complaint I have heard made against Charlton, the one which keeps him out of the lists when some people name the handful of the world's greatest players, is that he avoids the fury of the game, that where the hacking and elbowing are fiercest Charlton is not to be found. But this is like dismissing Dickens from the world's great literature because he never went to gaol for throwing bricks at politicians; like denigrating Disraeli on the grounds that he was a third-rate novelist. Charlton's courage is geared to his special talents. I have certainly never seen him fling himself headlong across his own goalmouth to head the ball away from some opposing forward's foot. But I have seen him summon his speed and use his swerve to score goals when defences were swinging their boots at him with intent to hurt. Charlton has been felled so often in his career that he could not possibly have stayed so compellingly in the game for so long if he lacked nerve. I do not object at all that he has never been sent off the field for kneeing someone in the groin.

It is true, I think, to say that although he became an England international player when he was 20 it was in later years that he gathered full resolution for the game. He was never less than an excellent player, but he was past 25 before he became a great one. He flowered fully, and gloriously, for the World Cup in 1966, appropriately scoring England's first goal with a veering run from near the centre-circle and a characteristic shot taken in mid-stride. He scored another like it in the semi-final against Portugal. They are the kind of goals he will be remembered by. They are a great player's goals.

Yet Charlton is not just a scoring specialist. Being so fast and possessing the best body swerve of his generation, he made his name as a winger. In his early years as a professional his great merit was his ability to run past the defender from the left touchline and go diagonally on the back's inside to hit the ball at goal with either foot. This was the young

Charlton, with most of his weight in his legs, whose speed and control of the ball were aimed exclusively at scoring goals. By his late 20s — he was 28 in the 1966 World Cup — he had moved to a deep-lying centre-forward or inside-forward position, as the fulcrum of the attack. His accuracy with the ball at great distance was now used to shift, in one sudden pass, the point of action. These passes, especially if preceded by one of his sidesteps and a burst of acceleration, could turn the fortune of a game instantly. A moment's work of this calibre from him, perhaps at the edge of his own penalty area, could take his side out of an alarming defensive situation and have it menacing the other goal immediately. I saw him do this once against Liverpool and the moment stunned that ferocious crowd into silence.

Charlton makes his own rules for dealing with a football. He is a player to admire but not for younger ones to copy. When he strikes the ball he often has his head up high, instead of looking down over the ball as the coaches teach. He will flick at it with the outside of his left foot when leaning back looking at the sky. When players on his own side are unaccustomed to him they often find that the ball comes to them, having miraculously been 'bent' round some obstructing opponent, spinning violently and therefore difficult to control; only the best can take advantage of such passes, as Denis Law, Best and Jimmy Greaves (in the international side) all have. Charlton does not dribble with the ball in the sense that Best does, patting it between his feet, nor does he run with it as if it is tied by elastic to him, as in the case of Pele, of Brazil, so that it bounces against his knees, thighs, stomach, ankles as he moves. Charlton kicks the ball close to the ground in front of him, often a long way in front, and runs like a sprinter behind it, almost as if there was no ball at all. No boy could possibly be taught such a method of playing football.

This run deceives defenders. They see the ball coming towards them, with Charlton well behind it, and they think they can reach it before him. Suddenly, just as they commit themselves, his right shoulder dips, his whole weight goes momentarily on his right foot, flat on the grass, and then he has sped past them the other way, kicking the ball in front of him as he goes. His own speed, coupled with the defender's impetus, often means that he is ten yards clear before the defender has turned. To be beaten by Charlton's swerve is to be beaten for good. If the defender anticipates the swerve and turns in the right direction Charlton will clear the tackle expertly like a hurdler.

Soccer

There is delicious exhilaration in watching movement like this. Crowds will him to repeat it, and if he gets the ball and pauses as if gathering himself for such a run the whole sound of the stadium changes from its baying and grumbling into an excited purr. If he decides the moment is not right, and releases the ball quickly with a merely sensible short pass, there is a deep groan of disappointment.

He has his bad matches, when his touch deserts him and the casual flicks and lobs skim away erratically, sometimes presenting the other team with the initiative they had lost. In games like these his shooting at goal can be laughably wild, and yet there is seldom laughter; the communal embarrassment is the same that settles around a wrong final note from the recital platform. Charlton hates these lapses. He reacts to them with something close to self-revulsion, like a man discovering a flea in his vest. He shakes his head wretchedly, apologizes to the company, and on his very worst days may keep clear of the ball for a while. More often he tries to compose himself, trapping the ball and striking it with an unusual, elaborate care. It is only now that he looks awkward. When Charlton is keeping his eye intently on the ball, as every good player is supposed to, then he is at his least effective. He is not a player's player, in the sense of being reliable, even though he is entirely professional in his attitude to the game; he is certainly a spectator's player, in the sense that he is a sight to watch.

From *The Football Man* by Arthur Hopcraft, published by William Collins Ltd. Reprinted by permission of the author.

Geoffrey Green

ONE HUNDRED YEARS OF CUP MAGIC
CHRISTMAS CARD JOGS A BRAZILIAN MEMORY
LIGHTNING STRIKES IN TURIN

Geoffrey Green was for many years Football Correspondent of the *Times*, a post he took up in 1946. He wrote official histories of the Football Association and the F.A. Cup, and a world survey of the game. He also wrote a volume on great moments in soccer, and an appraisal of the history of Manchester United.

He had great powers of recollection of the stirring scenes in his world-wide travels, and had a unique ability for recreating them vividly. He loved the English forward line of instinctive players in the post-war era, and was critical of the patterned defensive play of recent times.

ONE HUNDRED YEARS OF CUP MAGIC

It is 1871—mid-Victorian England; the age of Gladstone and Disraeli which saw the beginnings of social and industrial reform; the age of the horse and carriage; of the top hat and the cloth cap; of extravagant beards and mutton-chop whiskers; of Dickens. It is a period which brought the curtailment of long working hours and, more important, that unique social creation, the Saturday half-holiday.

When the age began comfortable men, as often as not, went to the City on Saturday afternoons. By the time it closed, a working carpenter at 2 pm on any Saturday might expect to be strolling round with his pipe to the Dog and Duck— or perhaps pushing his way into a crowd at a football match.

Those free Saturday afternoons did more than anything to make the game popular with all sections of the community. It was during this period, too, that football was for the first time fashioned from a chaos of varying rules and regulations into some semblance of order. There had, it is true, been earlier attempts at coordination, but the first enduring step in this direction came from the formation of The Football Association in 1863, so named because it was an association of clubs which held an identity of views and together set down a code of laws.

The story of the Cup, or, to give it its correct title, The Football Association Challenge Cup, opened eight years later. The date was July 20 and the scene a small, oak-panelled room at the office of *The Sportsman*, a London newspaper. There sat seven men dressed in the height of fashion as befitted their place in society, each a member of the best-known teams of that period.

The moving spirit was C.W. Alcock, secretary of The Football Association, about 30, born in Sunderland but schooled in the game at Harrow. Near him sat A. Stair, of the Upton Park Club, honorary treasurer of the FA Committee; C.W. Stephenson, of Westminster School; J.H. Giffard, of the Civil Service Club; D. Allport, of the Crystal Palace Football Club; M.P. Betts, of Harrow; and a young officer of the Royal Engineers, Captain (later Sir) Francis Marindin.

After the formal business had been dealt with, Alcock proposed: "That it is desirable that a Challenge Cup should be established in connexion with the association, for which all clubs belonging to the association should be invited to compete."

The idea was at once received with favour and at a subsequent meeting on October 16, 1871, the resolution was carried. Meanwhile the clubs had been invited to subscribe towards the purchase of the Cup, a modest enough trophy costing no more than £20.

Fifteen teams entered for the first competition and of these only two—Queen's Park, Glasgow, and Donington Grammar School—came from north of Hertfordshire. Hitchin, Royal Engineers, Reigate Priory, Maidenhead and Great Marlow were outside the metropolitan radius, but the other eight entries—Wanderers, Harrow Chequers, Barnes, Civil Service, Crystal Palace, Upton Park, Clapham Rovers and Hampstead Heathens—came fairly under the heading of London clubs.

Within the framework of those early years the great

amateur clubs and players of the South stood supreme, many of the players coming from the public schools and universities. They had borrowed the old game of mob football from the working people and reshaped it, but the people one day were to take it back again until finally football, from being the amusement of a leisured class, grew to be the sport of nations. The influence of the Cup in this change is incalculable, for the magic of the "little tin idol", as it was soon called, spread steadily across the fields of England, drawing more and more clubs under its spell. It altered the pattern of football, leading first to professionalism and then to the system of the Football League.

This year the FA Cup celebrates its centenary. Looking back along the lengthening mountain range of its varied, tumultuous life several high peaks stand out. It has had three major homes—first, the Kennington Oval from 1872 to 1892, where once Lord Kinnaird, of the flowing red beard and white flannel trousers, jumped for joy and stood on his head in front of the cricket pavilion as he gained his fifth cup-winning medal when his team, the Old Etonians, beat Blackburn Rovers in the final of 1882; next, the old Crystal Palace from 1893 to 1914, where in 1901 the first six-figure crowd in football history (110,820) saw Tottenham Hotspur play Sheffield United in the final; and now, Wembley.

At its opening in 1923 the stadium was invaded by a crowd estimated at some 200,000 to see Bolton Wanderers face West Ham United at the climax. The human tide swamped the pitch and the match — begun almost an hour late while King George V waited patiently in the Royal Box—was saved by the activities of "the policeman on the white horse", who went into history and until his death was annually presented with a complimentary Cup Final ticket.

There have also been three separate cups. The first — that "little tin idol"—was stolen on the night of September 11, 1895, from the shop window of William Shillcock, football boot manufacturer, of Newton Row, Birmingham. Never found again, its replica was awarded in 1910 to Lord Kinnaird on completion of his 21 years as president of the Football Association.

The third (and present) trophy, presented in 1910-11, is more handsome than its predecessors and it is after the style of an antique votive urn, 19in high, exclusive of plinth, weighing 175oz.

Aston Villa stand as the champions with seven victories over the years from their first triumph in 1887. They are

Soccer

followed by Newcastle United and Blackburn Rovers with six wins apiece. Whose turn is it for glory in this historic year?

From the *Times*, 6 May 1972.

CHRISTMAS CARD JOGS A BRAZILIAN MEMORY

It was a Christmas card from Brazil this week that triggered off memory. Three years ago England went there to take part in a four-cornered football tournament with Brazil, the hosts, Argentina and Portugal, a celebration that later came to be called the "little World Cup" by those who like tidy pigeon-holes.

As a trip to a people racially colourblind it was an eye-opener. Its contrasts were sharp—the jewel of Rio de Janeiro that hid beneath it the squalid *favellas*, the slums that fester without sanitation; the busy functionalism of São Paulo; the awful chasm between wealth and poverty; the tall, hot winds of Rio and the deafening clatter of a sudden tropical downpour; the sportsmanship and the gamesmanship. It was all there.

Friends had often spoken of the thrill of flying in over Rio, seeing in relief the white crested curve of its bay, the surrounding foliage as fresh as an Irish meadow and there, far below, the massive oval shape of Maracana Stadium, for all the world like some giant flying saucer at rest on earth, the national stage of Brazilian football which once held the record crowd of 200,000 for the World Cup final of 1950.

All this had fired imagination. With it, too, went the hope of one day seeing Brazil, champion footballers, in their daffodil shirts and bluebell shorts, take the field side by side with the white of England.

Covered by Cloud
The fates, however, were in a playful mood that day three years ago. Spanning the South Atlantic and the clock from supper in Paris to breakfast next morning in Rio, there was nothing on arrival to be seen of that gem beneath. Blanketed by seven-eighths cloud and a raging rainstorm, this might have been Manchester or Macclesfield for all we could guess. Even the taxi driver, blinded by the rain, had to stop his panting machine by the wayside from the airport to the hotel. Thus one dream—of seeing Rio for the first time from the air—had been pricked.

I retired for an afternoon siesta to repair the ravages of a sleepless journey.

Consciousness returned with a sudden, painful start. The room was pitch dark; the time just after 8 p.m. Thousands of miles across the world and here I had missed the eight o'clock kick-off. No Brazilian or English players would I now see marching out shoulder to shoulder. So the second dream had been exploded cruelly.

Endless Journey

Gripped by panic, and with a job to be done at all costs, somehow or other a taxi duly materialized. In the distance there was the white glow in the sky—the floodlights of Maracana. The taxi's radio crackled as the crowd roared and the names spluttered out tantalizingly—Pele, Julinho, Vava; Bobby Charlton, Greaves, Moore. What was happening? The driver, absorbed by the commentator's voice, drove hard, head down, but the lights refused to come nearer.

At last we were there. For a stranger to invade that fortress of Maracana Stadium alone for the first time is the saga of the Count of Monte Cristo in reverse. Like a rabbit caught in headlights, the victim ran on blindly. The hands of the watch said a quarter to nine: half time.

Suddenly, like a welcome lighthouse in fog, the faces of colleagues at last were gratefully sighted. Sinking into the press box I inquired shamefacedly of the half-time score. "Half-time?" came an angry chorus. "Go back to Europe. This is some foul trick of yours to get a good sleep. We've been sitting here for more than two hours and they haven't even started yet." At that precise moment the teams emerged side by side.

The Brazilians later claimed that their team coach had been delayed in a traffic accident. But there were those of the English press, inspecting the stadium earlier, who vowed they had stumbled across the hosts resting secretly within their fortress long before their opponents had arrived to sit changed and fretting in the visitors' dressing room.

Genuine accident, or a war of nerves and gamesmanship? We shall never really know. All that mattered, however, was that my second dream, by some strange chance, had been rescued. There, too, to be wondered at was the fanatical but sporting appreciation by 100,000 *aficionados* of England's play; and the magic sight of Maracana itself shimmering in its floodlights. Above shone a full moon; to one side, dominating the uppermost rim of the stadium, stood the famous golden statue of Christ, bathed in light, at the top of Corcovado mountain which broods over the city and the bay of flawless beauty.

At the end the whole scene was aflame with the bonfires of victory. Here was Carnival time, a mirror of the Brazilian film *Black Orpheus* on a night that belonged to Pele, the black diamond, as he bewitched England, a player worthy of such a setting.

First-time View

Some days later a padre at the British Embassy told how on returning from home leave he always came back to Rio by ship. "I make a point of going up on deck in the dawn as we steam quietly into the bay", he said. "It is a breathtaking sight, this jewel in its natural setting, with the Sugar Loaf mountain to one side and Corcovado, taller still, in the background.

"On my last trip I followed my usual practice. But on this occasion I found I was not alone. Leaning on the ship's rail was an elderly Brazilian who, it transpired, was seeing Rio for the first time. Noticing my dog-collar, he turned towards me and as thin tears trickled down his dark, lined face he pointed to Corcovado. 'Look at that old devil Christ', he said."

Devil or Christ; poverty or riches; gamesmanship or sportsmanship—Braziliana, with its Dionysiac dance, its colour, music and compulsion of drums, has it all for anyone, no matter his lot, who believes that every day can be Christmas Day if he wants it to be. But with it he also needs a bit of luck; and a Christmas card to stir memory.

From the *Times*, 23 December 1967.

LIGHTNING STRIKES IN TURIN

Then, in the bat of an eyelid, it happened. Wright came out of defence, brushing aside the pressure as he fed Matthews down the wing. A feint to the right, a swivel inwards to the left — and the maestro had left two defenders on the wrong foot. But instead of holding the ball close, searching for the next victim of his footwork as was his way, Matthews now suddenly released a long through pass some 40 yards ahead with his left foot, inside and beyond the Italian left back. He had spotted his partner, Mortensen moving ahead like the wind, along an inside-right course.

For Italy it proved to be a fatal, collision course. In a few more strides Mortensen was level with the pass, clear of the

Soccer

defence, still going like an express train, but in full command and perfectly balanced.

In a flash Parola saw the approaching danger. Leaving the centre of defence, he, too, moved fast to his left — aiming either to tackle, or at least to shepherd the intruder away towards the touchline. As Parola hit his man Mortensen had reached a point some three or four yards short of where the penalty area joins the goal line. But, fractionally before he was sent sprawling, 'Morty' released a piercing right foot arrow which miraculously bent into the top near corner of the Italian goal, a 'banana' shot which perhaps not even the great Pelé himself would have thought feasible from such an impossible angle and at such speed.

Out of darkness, through fire, into light. From having their backs desperately against the wall one second, the very next moment England found themselves one up — all in four minutes from the start! For their part, the Italians could scarcely believe their eyes. It was some mirage, surely. That huge crowd, packed tight in shirt sleeves like a white cloud in the shimmering light, grunted, caught its breath — and fell silent.

From *Great Moments in Sport: Soccer* by Geoffrey Green, published by Pelham Books Ltd.

John Moynihan

PARK SHOOTING

John Moynihan has written about the game for the *Observer*, the *Guardian*, and the *Sunday Telegraph*. In *The Soccer Syndrome* he traced the development of the game from the postwar era to success in the World Cup in 1966.

In his book, *Park Football*, he describes the joys of this improvised form of Soccer, which nevertheless conceals great ambitions. "Always we tried to emulate the feats of the Busby Babes, the Tottenham 'double' side, Real Madrid, England (1966)." After describing the arts of Park kicking and trapping, Park heading, Park dribbling and Park loitering ("hiding"), he turns his attention to the art of Park shooting, an essential skill.

PARK SHOOTING

Park shooting — Professional goalkeepers will tell you that the hardest shot to take is the mis-hit one; the one that bobs off a knee into the far corner or thumps against a thigh and rolls over the line.

Park footballers are brilliant at scoring with these efforts. This is the way we generally score. We might actually dream of scoring exquisite goals like Pele, Bobby Charlton and Jimmy Greaves from devastating distances and fantastic angles after beating four men but these magic moments are rare and when they happen a mood of sheer disbelief overwhelms the park. Genius is looked on with suspicion. Our efforts to put the ball between the sticks or coats are essentially plebeian but gone about with monumental industry and lack of reward.

I've seen five attackers stretched along the goal line with the ball at their feet and the goalkeeper on the ground and between them they've been unable to put 'dirty leather

Soccer

in net'. Why, for goodness sake, why? Well, to start with they've all tried to put the ball in themselves and, in knocking each other off the ball, have exhausted and destroyed their raging efforts to equalise. The ball has just sat there waiting to be thumped like a true masochist and nothing has happened.

The weirdest goal I saw in our standard of football was on the playing fields of Eton when Chelsea Casuals played the old boys. Two of the Casuals forwards dribbled the ball into the Etonian penalty area together but in their haste to knock each other off the ball with two grubby Kings Road hands only managed to overbalance their duet. At last they succeeded in hitting the ball into goal with two toe caps locked together. 'Rotten form,' said a pink-cheeked Eton 'keeper.

The intrinsic thing to remember about scoring goals in the park is never to listen to your colleagues when you're in a cosy position to shoot. They will do their best to get the ball away from you. They will ravish you with advice, mostly feeble, about when to open fire. Some of them will even advise you not to shoot.

'Don't shoot,' I heard one frenzied inside-forward roar at me when I was one yard from the line with the ball at my feet. I pulled up, looked back and the goalkeeper scooped the ball off my toes. It is better to wear ear plugs.

One way of getting goals is to make faces at the goalkeeper while he is taking goal kicks in deep mud. Park goalkeepers can't kick the ball very far and when they see your face pulled over on to one cheek, like a bowl of steaming ravioli, they might slice the ball straight to your feet.

From *Park Football* by John Moynihan, published by Pelham Books Ltd. Reprinted by permission of Irene Josephy.

Rugby Union

David Irvine
THE JOY OF RUGBY

David Irvine, a Rugby and Lawn Tennis commentator for the *Guardian*, in his lavishly illustrated book, *The Joy of Rugby*, describes the game as "a glorious hotch-potch", tries to characterise its present-day appeal, and claims that it has as its distinguishing component pure fun, the concept of communal enjoyment.

From THE JOY OF RUGBY

Basing an understanding of Rugby on a visit to Twickenham, however, was -- and still is — like expecting an American visitor to understand Britain and the British on the strength of a day trip to Stratford-on-Avon. Twickenham and Stratford are merely showpieces. The real Britain, and the real game of Rugby Football, is a glorious hotch-potch, offering an infinite variety of traditions, styles and national and regional peculiarities, and appealing to men (and women) from all parts of the social spectrum. Even today some people may still be tempted to think in terms of a typical 'rugger type'; thankfully the vast majority now accept that Rugby Football is a game for all kinds and conditions. And for this the game owes a considerable debt to the influence of television.

Like all sports, rugby is knee-deep in clichés and, in choosing a title like *The Joy of Rugby* it would be very easy to fall into the trap of over-sentimentalising the game. Any team activity played with real skill, ambition and purpose by players who have attained a high degree of fitness and a proper command of the basic requirements, must offer a real feeling of joy and satisfaction. Rugby does not hold a monopoly in such matters. Unlike a professional team sport like soccer, though, rugby is play, not work. Nor does it begin and end with a blast from a referee's whistle. It may be true to say that there is probably a greater emphasis today on winning (is that necessarily suspect?) but so far there has been no sign that this has impaired the real fellowship which is the game's valued foundation.

In many respects the way the game is played has changed out of recognition in the past 15 or 20 years, which is why this book is so often concerned with this crucial period in rugby's development. And yet is the end result so very different? The competitive element may be stronger, horizons may have broadened and organisation may have risen to new levels but thousands still give of their time and effort without reward just as their forefathers did. Men like these will not be counted among those with no idea how to fill increasing leisure hours. Rugby has developed and thrived in the hands of such men for more than 150 years because humour, grief, happiness, fellowship and the desire to win — all component parts of the human character — have been so effectively encompassed on the rugby field.

Rugby's greatest characteristic, though, is that while it is taken seriously by its followers, it is never taken solemnly. Fun keeps bursting in. And the impression that rugby fun is merely another way of describing wild excesses of overgrown schoolboys is one which, in the following chapters, I hope to refute along with the belief that the game itself is the preserve of a chosen minority.

. . . . . .

What ultimately influences anyone's approach to the game, then, is what he expects to get out of it. For the vast, unpublicised majority, the aim is modest, simple and entirely within the avowed intentions of the game's earliest administrators — exercise and enjoyment. Although playing to win is their objective, winning is not everything. Those who want more (fame, success, even perfection) must give more: of their time and their energies. And the rewards can be considerable, not least for those who attain the highest levels and are offered the opportunity of travelling the world at someone else's expense.

Superficially there may be a tendency, particularly in an age in which so much of our life is conditioned by, and dependent upon, advanced technology, to view rugby in overtechnical terms. Yet the essential qualities which capture and

Rugby Union

sustain players' loyalties are very simple. Perhaps it is understandable that only those who have played, from the humblest schoolboy beginner to the most celebrated international, fully appreciate what rugby means to its devotees. The uninitiated observer sees sixteen hulking forwards fighting for a ball in ankle-deep mud and wonders at their sanity. Yet in many ways the scrum represents the very heart and soul of the game, and the sweat, the pain, the aching limbs and bursting lungs that go to make up the scrum are what earn rugby its unique place among the world's great games. For no other sport remains so civilised while involving its players in such constant, close and fierce bodily contact.

But even at its most rustic level rugby is not merely an 80-minute interlude to be taken once a week. The game itself is only a beginning. Loyalties and friendships forged in those scrums will and do stand the test of time and are among rugby's most cherished rewards. If winning is the principal objective, losing is rarely regarded as justification for sulking, enmity or serious and lasting disagreement.

. . . . . .

Although in many ways a ready-made vehicle for violence, rugby is generally conducted with self-control and good humour with the unwritten laws observed even more meticulously than the written. It has never been easy to persuade those outside the game that there is a clear distinction between 'rough' and 'dirty' play but players generally recognise the different categories and those who cross the line of demarcation do so consciously and in full awareness of the penalties.

Rugby would wither rapidly were 'The Spirit' not observed and, while it would be foolish to pretend that there are not some who operate beyond the laws, the general behaviour pattern would seem to accept the limits which have evolved over more than a century of playing. Wavell Wakefield likened rugby to war — but it is still a war without weapons. The threat of injury is no deterrent and, if anything, the challenge and element of danger which the game provides is one of the attractions in a social climate where cosiness and complacency increasingly abound.

From *The Joy of Rugby* by David Irvine, published by William Luscombe.

Carwyn James

A YOUNG ROMANTIC REDISCOVERS SOME OF HIS OLD POETRY

Carwyn James has earned fame as a Welsh outside-half, and as the first man to coach a victorious Lions' team this century. He is Rugby Correspondent of B.B.C. Wales and writes often for the *Guardian*. With John Reason he wrote *The World of Rugby*, a history of Rugby Union football from its earliest days. He is a penetrating analyst of the game, and an admirer of versatility, and so of the virtuoso Mike Gibson.

A YOUNG ROMANTIC REDISCOVERS SOME OF HIS OLD POETRY

Mike Gibson, a born fly half who became a centre three-quarter played his best ever rugby in New Zealand in 1971, where, it seems, he rediscovered the game of his youth and perhaps, even more important, he rediscovered himself in the play of Barry John.

I have the delightful vision of the young romantic undergraduate at Cambridge who, by allowing his natural instincts the freedom of Grange Road, thrilled the critics, the dons and such perceptive diagnostics as Dr Windsor-Lewis. For a young man in love with rugby football — "it is a game of touch and feel and instinct" — it was the perfect honeymoon and it lasted just about as long. Then gradually the enquiring uneasy mind took over and it led to the search for the reasons why, borne of the fear of trusting the romantic imagination. Reading law rather than literature may well have accelerated the process for Mike Gibson.

After Cambridge, in Gibson's Ireland, analysis and the

thought processes which could be controlled became more important than imagination and flair. In Irish rugby, as in Sir Alf Ramsey's parochial domain, the mid-sixties was a period of analysis, of seeking first principles, of laying far more stress on defence, destruction and safety rather than on risking any means of attack. Ireland, perhaps more than any other country in the post-1966 period, became the disciples of the New Zealand pattern, and the lofted kicks of Barry McGann, and the attacking defence of Gibson plus any veteran centre, became the main forms of attack. For a time, at least, it suited the Irish temperament, a case of a predictable approach leading to the unpredictable.

The period of analysis led Mike Gibson to think deeply about his game. He accepted the idea that the skills of the game, the ordinary habits of life, have to be practised so well that they become second nature to a player and they never enter the conscious mind. The mind is liberated to think on other more important things, more particularly, to assess the options or the possibilities offered to a player in a given situation.

Assessing the options means deep concentration: "At international level I only feel satisfied if I come off the field feeling mentally tired." In this context his passion for golf leads Mike Gibson to talk of Tony Jacklin and Gary Player. He recalls how Jacklin in the early part of the American golf circuit of 1972 was leading the field with only five holes to play and yet contrived to finish in fifth place. Jacklin lost his concentration, his single-mindedness: "I choked. I was walking up the 13th fairway and I suddenly became aware of the spectators watching me and expecting me to win." He recalls how Player won the British Open in spite of being in intense pain. The triumph of mind over matter.

In a keen game concentration means an appreciation of the opposition, and the discovery of weaknesses. It also leads to the kind of patience necessary to play the waiting game and lulling the opposition into a state of relaxation which is synonymous with losing concentration.

Touring South Africa with the Lions in 1968, Gibson by then a keen student of the game, was anxious to put his considered theories into practice. I recall Cliff Morgan telling me of his surprise when he discovered on an internal flight how his travelling companion was completely engrossed in his reading of dozens of set moves and their counters which he, Gibson, had written out in his own hand. Morgan, a natural himself and a great admirer of Gibson, was tempted to tell him to burn the lot. The young romantic undergraduate had researched to doctorate proportions and his game in the process had become clinical and contrived. In poetical terms the young Coleridge had become an Alexander Pope or a Dryden.

For a number of seasons Gibson had borne the pressures demanded by Ireland at the international level and his game was entirely the product of the intellect and the conscious level. In 1971 the intense young man relaxed. Alongside him he had Barry John and he had John Dawes: "His choice of play was as immaculate as his use of the ball." And outside him, the wings: "Imagine how I felt as a midfield player knowing that I had only to create an extra foot of space for Gerald and he would capitalize on it!" Behind him, J.P.R. Williams: "One of the features of the Lions' attacking play was the creation of the overlap and we found that John Williams opened new horizons for full back play by his incursions into the line."

In Barry John he found a kindred soul: "I certainly found that by playing alongside him my vision became broader. Above all, he was the player who personified the attitude of the team." Caring for one's own game more than worrying about what the opposition is going to do means composure and the complete relaxation which only comes through intense concentration before a match. Barry John sat in a corner of the dressing-room before a game in complete silence, his eyes and ears closed to the world and to the team talk immensely capable of a complete, meditative self-motivation. Such a positive attitude breathes confidence, sometimes even a touch of brashness. A player may create a state of mind in which he is greater than he himself.

To return to Jacklin and the strange concept that very occasionally a sportsman may mysteriously sense that he is completely in control of a moment: "When I'm in this state everything is pure, vividly clear. I'm in a cocoon of concentration. And if I can put myself into that cocoon, I'm invincible."

Of Mike Gibson it has been said that he has the power of total recall. For most of the time this is entirely true. But I think I have witnessed moments in his game, at a different level of perception, which are above total recall. His career, it seems to me, has come full circle. By hard work at the skills of the game, by playing a completely relaxed game in the company of such great players as Barry John, he has rediscovered the romantic imagination of his youth, which

Rugby Union

few players have ever achieved. I can think of no better tribute to the greatest centre three-quarter the modern game of rugby football has produced. That he never played in any of the Test matches in South Africa last summer hurt rugby football more than it hurt Mike Gibson.

From the *Guardian*, 14 March 1975.

David Frost

BARRY JOHN'S THREE GIFTS

David Frost has been a lively commentator on Rugby for the *Guardian* for many years, and in one of his books gave a striking account of the New Zealand tour of the British Isles and France in 1967.

Here he assesses the skills of Barry John, the "King", who ascended his "throne" in New Zealand in 1971.

BARRY JOHN'S THREE GIFTS

The achievements of Barry John, who has announced his retirement from rugby, seem destined to have an extensive influence on the game as a whole. Just as his career was divided into three distinct stages, so his influence on the game's future is likely to be threefold.

At the start of his career he was known chiefly as a gifted and accurate tactical kicker. Gradually his reputation broadened, and he became acknowledged as a subtle runner. The third stage was not reached until the 1970-71 season when he took over the place-kicking for Cardiff. Immediately he added the fresh and priceless dimension of goalkicking to his play.

On the 1971 Lions' tour of New Zealand these three facets of his game united to make him the master player. No opposing full back can have been more mercilessly teased and tortured than was Fergi McCormick in the first Test by the raking punts that rolled off Barry John's boot. No more breathtaking individual try was ever scored than John's against the New Zealand Universities, the try which took his total of points for the tour beyond a hundred. Until John scored 188 no goalkicker on tour in New Zealand had ever scored more than 100 points.

It was this triumphant Lions' tour that placed Barry John in a position from which to influence the game far and wide. His first contribution, which may prove the most lasting,

Rugby Union

was the unorthodoxy of his delivery of the ball to his inside centre. Orthodoxy requires a stand-off half to take a pace inwards in passing so as to straighten the line of attack. Close observers of Barry John in New Zealand noted that after handing the ball on quickly—he moved off immediately in the direction of the pass.

The straightening of the line of attack was left to the centres, John Dawes and Mike Gibson, who were ideally equipped to do it. By quickly moving out across the field Barry John was well placed to start a counter-attack if the ball went loose and was booted through by the Lions' opponents; or he could lend immediate support if the Lions' movement was checked on the wing; and he was out of the reach of heavy-tackling loose forwards who have maimed too many stand-off halves.

John, who had suffered numerous injuries earlier in his career—he missed most of the 1968 Lions' tour of South Africa because of a broken collarbone—came through New Zealand virtually unscathed. His technique of delivery and subsequent positional play may well become a model for the stand-off halves of the future.

John's second contribution was the manner in which he accepted fame and adulation without becoming spoilt by them. Both in New Zealand and in Britain since his return he has been a popular hero worshipped by his public. By steering a level-headed and friendly course through all the clamour and publicity he has set a clear example for future stars to follow.

Thirdly, there is his round-the-corner goalkicking. John was by no means the first man to use this method, even in international rugby. But before he started kicking goal after goal in New Zealand, there was generally thought to be something freakish about this method, and it was held to be inaccurate. John was successful with 20 of his first 24 attempts at conversions in New Zealand. He passed his 100 points in his first eight matches.

The influence of all this has already been seen. Before the end of that Lions' tour, local schoolboy goalkickers were to be seen using the round-the-corner method in curtain-raisers on the Lions' match days. It would be no great surprise if a future All-Black touring team—perhaps next season's All Blacks in Britain—were to produce a kicker using this method. Even John Dawes was observed taking round-the-corner goalkicks in the Middlesex Sevens at Twickenham last week.

From the *Guardian*, 9 May 1972.

Michael Green

K IS FOR KICKER

Michael Green wrote *The Art of Coarse Rugby* in 1960, and it was so successful that he followed up with a series. These covered Rugby itself once again, sailing, amateur dramatics and golf. He has contributed regularly to the *Sunday Times*, and has broadcast.

In *Michael Green's Rugby Alphabet*, which covers the whole spectrum of the game, K, we find, is for Kicker.

K IS FOR KICKER

Because kicking is so neglected, most players are hardly aware of the subtle difference between the many types of kick, such as the screw-kick which floats into touch, and its opposite number which curves infield at the vital moment. There are, however, different bad kicks which will be instantly recognisable.

The most common is the Hoop-la. This is frequently seen in suburban meadows, but is not unknown at Murrayfield or Twickenham. In this, the kicker steadies himself carefully, waits until the opposition are nearly on him and then very carefully, and with tremendous force, kicks the ball backwards over his own head. With luck, his own full-back may catch it, but more often the other side gets there first.

A variation of this is the Yellow Streak. It is the kick made by the team's coward, who must get rid of the ball at all costs. The kicker starts his kick even before he has received the pass, and usually strikes it with his knee, whereupon the ball soars vertically upwards while the kicker runs for cover, burying his head in his arms.

Another frequently-seen kick is, of course, the Non-Starter, in which the kicker misses the ball altogether. I've done it frequently myself and I don't know a more embarrassing thing on the rugby field. The worst of it is that the momentum of kicking swings you round and you fall flat on your back while the ball bounces tantalisingly by your side, until some opponent seizes it gleefully. The only way of dodging a storm of abuse from your own side is instantly to feign an injured ankle, but even that will probably do little to protect you.

Forwards seem to have their own special type of kick (The Grunt). It has always been a mystery to me why some sixteen stone second-row forward, with legs like young oak trees, is only capable of feebly disturbing the ball when he has to kick it. Usually the ball travels in a tiny parabola for about three feet. You would think he'd be ashamed of himself, but oh dear no. After making a kick like this most forwards give a sheepish grin and go 'Huh, huh, huh' to show that really they're not supposed to know how to kick and that it was jolly sporting of them even to try.

Place-kicking, too, has as many variations.

First, there's the Patella Fracture, in which the kicker stares mesmerised at the ball for some twenty seconds, slowly advances upon it, and then buries the toe of his boot six inches in the soil about a foot in front of it. To make matters worse, he then usually hops about on one leg voiding himself of yelps of agony, and may even retire from the field injured.

Then there's the Toppler. This isn't really a kick at all, since the ball refuses to stand up and be kicked. After the third time it falls over, the unhappy kicker is driven desperate by the jeers and groans of both sides and usually makes a wild stab at the ball as it lies at a drunken angle on the ground. Just occasionally, the ball actually goes over the bar, after describing a sort of corkscrew parabola.

If this should happen, the kicker inevitably walks back with an air of great modesty, muttering something about, 'A lot of the greatest kickers prefer to place the ball at an angle . . . no, honestly, I meant to put it like that, it wasn't an accident . . .' etc. etc. Probably the greatest importance of the Toppler which goes over is the moral effect on the opposition, who are reduced to impotent silence, varied by occasional cries of 'Gawd'.

As one who has himself had the rare distinction of completely missing the ball in a place-kick, my own favourite variation is the Gurdoink, in which the kicker charges fran-

Rugby Union

tically at the ball, lifts his head at the last minute and scrapes his studs along the upper surface of the ball. As I say, in moments of stress, the ball may be missed altogether, but this is a connoisseur's piece.

From *Michael Green's Rugby Alphabet* by Michael Green, published by Pelham Books Ltd.

J.B.G. Thomas
JARRETT'S MATCH

J.B.G. Thomas is one of the foremost writers on Rugby, and one of its chief historians. He conveys his great enthusiasm through his books, with their non-sensational style and careful reporting. He has travelled all over the world to watch Rugby encounters, and gives faithful reports of the greatest moments, with their heroes, from his abundant memory.

"Jarrett's Match" is the twenty-third chapter of *Great Moments in Sport*.

JARRETT'S MATCH

Cardiff Arms Park, April 15, 1967.

Wales 34 pts. England 21 pts.

Now, here was a day! One to remember, and described by the *Playfair Rugby Annual* as the 'Most remarkable international match of all time'. Not quite, perhaps, but certainly remarkable, and certainly memorable. For Keith Jarrett, it could remain the highlight of a short but colourful career, as it was *his* day. The day when he made a dream debut; one that even a novelist could not improve upon or indeed conjure. It had everything for this young man, only four months out of school.

England had a good side which had beaten Ireland and Scotland and was in line for the Triple Crown and Championship. With less than 15 minutes remaining for play, they were only four points in arrears and going well. Then, only eight minutes later, they were 19 points in arrears before finishing strongly to end the match in defeat but with the remarkable final tally of 34-21. Had this happened in the 1930's it would have been regarded as stuff and nonsense but it was to herald a phenomenal run of high scoring in matches between the two countries. In seven from 1967 to 1973, Wales scored 151 points to England's 72, and this averaged 34 points a match by the two countries.

Thus this one launched a new era. It is true that Wales won six and drew one of the seven matches but never before, at least not since 1914, had there been such open play between the two countries. When, against Wales, would England expect to score 21 points and not win, as in this match? When, as in 1969, would you expect Wales to score 30 points against England? Little wonder that TV viewers called it 'Rugby Spectacular' as both countries attacked, and there were times when England threatened victory, as in 1970, and led at half time, only for Wales to recover and pull the match out of the fire.

Yet it was Jarrett's match! This 18 year old, 6 ft. tall, 13 stone player left Monmouth School, a true nursery of the game, a few days before Christmas and was chosen for Newport's 1st XV as a centre and in his 16 matches scored 109 points. He had played in the fullback position at school between the ages of 14 and 16 and was also an outstanding young cricketer who, with Tony Jorden of England, was the mainstay of the rugby and cricket teams at Monmouth. Son of a former Warwickshire cricketer, he was a tall, handsome young figure as he took the field with the Welsh XV.

His selection was a gamble; for although he had promise, and skill, he was, at the time, young and untried in the 'big league'. Indeed, Jarrett was the youngest player to be capped by Wales at fullback, following Lewis Jones, Terry Davies and Terry Price, all capped when 19 years of age. In the week before the match, Newport played him at fullback at the request of the national selectors in a match against Newbridge, but quickly moved him back to centre as he was unhappy out of position!

Had he not already been selected for Wales, it is doubtful whether he would have been risked at fullback, but with three senior Newport players in the Welsh side, he was suitably encouraged and one of them, David Watkins, was leading the side in this his last International, although no one appreciated it at the time, not even the player himself!

As Jarrett commented after the match, 'I was nervous at the start but once I had kicked the first penalty goal (after nine minutes) I felt fine and realised I had made it. Having been picked as a kicker, I knew that if it went over, all would

Rugby Union

be well although I dread to think what would have happened had I failed! Yet I am still a little dazed by it all.'

The ball actually crossed over the bar after hitting the far upright from 30 yards, and after 17 minutes Wales went further ahead when Raybould dropped a goal. Hosen dropped out from his '25' line and the ball ricocheted off a Welsh forward high into the air for Raybould to gather and calmly line up a drop at goal from 45 yards. Then he let fly with his left foot and over went the ball, high between the posts!

England hit back with a try, the first of eight scored in this remarkable match. Outside half Finlan started the movement which was supported by Taylor and Rogers, before Barton dived over for the try that Hosen could not convert. Immediately afterwards, Keith Savage on the wing fell offside and Jarrett kicked his second penalty from 35 yards at a wide angle. Soon it was 14-3 after Wales had scored their first try through David Morris who dived on a wild pass from Pickering that sailed over the English line and Jarrett kicked an easy goal.

In injury time Hosen kicked a penalty goal from 30 yards for England after a late tackle and, at the interval, it was 14-6. Hosen followed with his second penalty when play restarted from 35 yards for a Welsh scrum infringement, and it was 14-9, only for Wales to hit back again with their second try. An England pass went astray for the second time and John Lloyd gathered it smartly to send an overhead pass to Gerald Davies. He handed on to Dewi Bebb who shot away from the clutches of Keith Savage.

Away went Bebb, drawing the covering defence with him, and then sent the ball inside to Gerald Davies who simply whizzed along to cross the line near the posts for a splendid try that Jarrett converted. By this time the crowd was awakened to a full state of enthusiasm and excitement with the best yet to come at 19-9.

England challenged again with a text book try achieved by a fine back movement that saw Danny Hearn provide Savage with an overlap and the wing raced over in the corner. Then Hosen kicking every bit as well as Jarrett, landed another penalty, a beauty from the touch line, 27 yards out to make it 19-15 and the match was wide open again, suggesting that the next side to score would stake a real claim to victory.

The stage was set for something sensational and Jarrett was the player to provide it, as it was becoming increasingly clear to all that this was his afternoon. He could do no wrong and, as they say . . . 'His next trick appeared impossible!'

Rugby Union

Colin MacFadyean kicked to the right touch line in an attempt to clear but the ball fell short and bounced high infield. There was no one, attacker or defender, near it and as Jarrett galloped towards it, the ball hung in the air. He was now a centre, hungry for the ball, and he got it and simply kept on running after gathering. This was it . . . he was bound to succeed and score . . . it just had to be . . . it was his day!

Keith Savage came in to meet Jarrett but he slipped the wing when he was still 40 yards or more from the England line. On, on, he went to dive over in the corner for a super try, only the second scored by a Welsh fullback in an international match . . . the first was Vivian Jenkins against Ireland in 1934 at Swansea. Then to prove he was the new young master, Jarrett kicked a superb conversion off the touch line!

Wales got another try when the forwards won a tight head scrum through good work by Norman Gale and his props, and Gareth Edwards dashed to the blindside. He handed on to Dewi Bebb who twisted out of a tackle and dived over and again the young master converted to make it 29-15. By this time England must have thought they had been engulfed by a red avalanche and yet another try, the fifth by Wales, came from Gerald Davies finishing off good approach work by flankers Morris and Taylor and, yes, this too was converted by Jarrett with his seventh goal of the match!

Wales at 34-15 had won the match and the tremendous surge of 15 points in eight minutes had snuffed out the England challenge, but England still had plenty of fight left and proved it by collecting another six points with a fourth penalty from Hosen and a second try from Barton to make it 34-21.

A remarkable match had ended, and its exciting course of action had created a new rugby hero, and a young man, not yet 19 years of age had claimed a place in the record books by scoring 19 points in his first international. For ever it would be known as Jarrett's match and his try was truly a great moment in it!

From *Great Moments in Sport* by J.B.G. Thomas, published by Pelham Books Ltd.

Richard Llewellyn
ON THE MOUND

Richard Llewellyn wrote his famous first novel, *How Green Was My Valley*, in 1939. It describes the boyhood of Huw Morgan among a small South Wales mining community.

The extract is from the chapter entitled "On the Mound". The love of the everyday things of life among the peace of the valleys shows clearly in this description of the Welsh national game.

ON THE MOUND

Ivor went on to referee and spin the coin, and when we won the end with the wind a big cheer went up, for the wind always dropped low toward sunset, so what there was of it, we would have for the first half.

A healthy sound is the tamp of the leather ball on short green grass and pleasant indeed to watch it rise, turning itself lazily, as though it were enjoying every moment of the trip up there, against blue sky, and coming down against the green, in a low curve right into the ready hands of a back.

A whistle from Ivor, and the captain on the other side takes his run and kicks, and as you watch the ball climb you see the teams running into position to meet one another underneath it.

A forward has it, but before he can so much as feel it properly, he is flat on his back, and the two sides are packing over him. A whistle from Ivor, and the first scrum, and shouts for Davy as he lifts his arms to bind his front men. In goes the ball and the tight, straining muscles are working, eight against eight, to hold one another and then push each other the length of the field, but the ball comes free behind the pack and their fly-half has it so fast that nobody knows till he is on his way toward our touch line with his three-quarters strung behind him and nothing but our full-back in his way. Shout, crowd, shout, with one voice that is long-drawn, deep, loud, and full of colour, rising now as the fly runs pell-mell and Cyfartha Lewis dances to meet him, and up on a rising note, for inches are between them, louder with the voice in an unwritten hymn to energy and bravery and strength among men.

But Cyfartha is like a fisherman's net. The fly has been too clever. He should have passed to his wing long ago but he is greedy and wants the try himself, and on he goes, tries to sell a dummy, and how the crowd is laughing now, for to sell a dummy to Cyfartha is to sell poison to a Borgia. The fly is down and Cyfartha kicks the ball half-way down the field to our forwards, and has time to offer his hand to poor Mr. Fly, who is bringing himself to think what happened after the mountain fell on him.

And my father is laughing so much that his glasses are having trouble to settle on his nose. Owen and Gwilyn are shouting for all they are worth, for Davy has the ball and his forwards are all round him to push through the enemy. Shoulders and knees are hard at work, men are going down, men stumble on top of them, fall headlong and are pinned by treading, plunging boots. Red and green jerseys are mixed with yellow and white, and mud is plenty on both. On, on, an inch, two inches, bodies heave against bodies, hands grab, legs are twisted, fall and crawl, push and squirm, on, on, there are the white posts above you, but red and green jerseys hide the line and form a wall that never shows a gap. On, yellow and white, pack up behind and keep close, pull the ball into the belly and shield it with your arms, down with your head, more shoulder from the pack, keep closer at the sides, push now, push, push, push. A red and green down in front, another, who carries away a third. Another push now, and the ball is slipping from him. A hand has come from the press below and grasps with the strength of the drowning, but a wriggle to the side and a butt with the hip loosens it and on, on, half an inch more, with an ankle tight in the fist of red and green who lies beneath two yellow and white and only enough of sense and breath to hang on.

Down with the ball now, full flat, with eight or nine on top of you, and there is the whistle.

The ball rests an inch over the line.

Then see the hats and caps go into the air, and hear a

shouting that brings all the women to the doors up and down the Hill, and some to lean from the back windows.

Again the whistle and Maldwyn Pugh looks up at the posts, makes his lucky sign, and takes his run at the ball that rests in its heeled mark and kept there by the hand of Willie Rees, who lies full length in the mud with his face turned away, not to be blinded by the slop that will come when the boot leaves his hand empty.

Empty it is, and the ball on its way, and the crowd quiet, with the quiet that is louder than noise, when all eyes are on the same spot and all voices tuned for the same shout.

The ball travels high, drops in a curve, turns twice. The crowd is on its way to a groan, but now the wind takes it in its arms and gives it a gentle push over the bar, no need for it, but sometimes the wind is a friend, and there it is.

We are a try and a goal, five points, to the good.

From *How Green Was My Valley* by Richard Llewellyn, published by Michael Joseph Ltd.

Alun Richards

THE TEMPLATE

In 1980 Alun Richards (born in South Wales in 1929), the prolific novelist and playwright, scripted the B.B.C. Wales' film celebrating the Welsh Rugby Union's centenary. In conjunction with this he wrote *A Touch of Glory*, a history of these hundred years in which he describes the evolution of the characteristic Welsh approach to the game, the mould that formed its style. The highlight of rugby he believed was seen in the Barbarians' fixture in 1973 against the Seventh All Blacks.

Carwyn James, who wrote the Afterword to the book, agreed that the chief glory of the Welsh game had been in half-back play, with its many instinctive players, and saw in Phil Bennett's try in that game "the true spirit of rugby football . . . the unique moment when the game almost assumes an art form".

THE TEMPLATE

The classic fly-halves like Glyn Davies or Barry John made everything look easy, whereas Morgan* sometimes left you with the impression that he might have damaged himself in the process. But when the spring unwound it was just as dynamic, and on balance he was a more effective player than any of his predecessors, reaching heights on the hard dry grounds of South Africa which went unseen at home. Carwyn James, a High Churchman, was one of his rivals but they were never seriously in contention, for Morgan's partnership with Rex Willis was a perfect understanding and of all the half-back combinations since the war, this one must rate as the

---

*Cliff Morgan, an outside-half, with a dynamic break and strong kick. He now controls outside sports' T.V. for the B.B.C.

equal of any. Of all his successors David Watkins was most like him, equally effective on occasions but never quite achieving the rapport with a partner which Morgan did. Phil Bennett, as great a kicker as Cleaver on his day, was another amalgam of the talents. What is extraordinary is that such players appear again and again, each one bringing familiar traits, each one special, and when they achieve the rapport with a partner that brings the best out of both, games come alight as they have always done. Half-backs, more than any other position, have been touched by glory since the best of them have displayed that instinctive Welsh flair which makes our rugby football at its best so distinctive. You can value them for many things: for the way they beat men, for the way they link up with their three-quarters, for their incisive knowledge of the precise moment to kick or to pass, or for their saving graces in defence. Anyone who saw Phil Bennett's last kick in the famous match between Llanelli and the 1972 All Blacks will remember it with special pleasure, for Bennett has that air of frailty which is typical of many Welsh halves, and the sight of him driving back opponents twice his size is part of the real thrill of rugby football, the kind of contest which distinguishes it from any other game. That day, in a cauldron of endeavour, his role was that of a kicking half, placing his kicks to cause the utmost confusion, selecting a long penalty punt to hover over Grant Batty, the fiery New Zealand wing, seconds after he had come on to the field as a replacement, testing him in exactly the same way as he had tested Joe Karam, the young fullback, in the opening minutes of the game. The pressure was on from the beginning, and Bennett's boot was eloquent in attack and defence, his last forty-yard kick a clearance that capped a faultless performance of courage and skill, and which was enhanced by the service he got all afternoon from his partner 'Chico' Hopkins who played his finest game on that occasion. In a strange way, these partnerships where one partner dominates the other give more pleasure than when giants are paired, possibly because the sight of a small scrumhalf giving his all is a greater test of the man than the effortless sophistication of a master. Bennett, like Cliff Morgan, played some of his best games on the hard, dry grounds of South Africa but unlike Morgan, his skills remain encapsulated on film. They both displayed at times the hunted, despairing quality which made their breaks all the more defiant—a reaction to circumstances which forced them to take control and seize initiatives from unusual positions.

Rugby Union

Both of them made things look more difficult than did Barry John who had an effortless style. Where Bennett worked, John glided, but both were splendid defensive players, finding in Edwards the kind of partner who gave them room to move which would have made them superb in any era of the game. Edwards' greatest achievement was not just the massive stamp he could put on the game by his own crackerjack athleticism, but his decisive role in these two partnerships which blossomed both for Wales and two successful Lions tours to New Zealand and South Africa.

. . . . . .

The template had not changed, but in the 1970s there was a coming together of all the talents which, aided by the changes in the laws and the creation of the squad system under a national coach, blossomed forth into the most spectacular era of all. We were now in the age of the superstar, and only New Zealand could claim superiority in a clutch of hard-fought games which avenged the most famous game of all. These games were, however, remarkable from the Welsh point of view in that one ingredient was missing, a demonstration of Welsh flair. With all the preparations and the intensity of coaching, it is ironic that previous victorious matches were always characterised by that genius who seized an opportunity to make something out of nothing. It might be the bustling industry of Cliff Morgan, or Clem Thomas' brilliant cross kick in 1953, or Wilf Wooller's dummy scissors in 1935, but of late, while the excitement was always present, few could emulate Jack Manchester, the New Zealand captain's remark in 1935, 'I never played in such a thrilling game.' It was left to the Barbarians and the All Blacks to re-create that game in 1973, a game of all the talents when the result became secondary to the quality of play and when the adventurous approach of both teams made a nonsense of parochial considerations, an omen perhaps for the future. We provided the ground, the captain and some of the players, but the inspiration was with the Barbarians and a New Zealand team who forgot their cares after an arduous tour. More than a touch of glory, this game was all glory, and rugby football was the victor.

From the Afterword, by Carwyn James

. . . like Alun Richards I believe that the jewel in the Welsh crown has always been half-back play and, with it, an expression of that flair which comes from the presence of so many instinctive players. Most of us remember the Barbarians' first try against the Seventh All Blacks. I remember it not only for its technical skill in the arts of passing, or the excellent support work and continuity of its execution, but for its spirit, its challenge, the defiance of the opposition from a hopelessly defensive situation. I can see it now and the impression is indelible.

A rolling ball, still rolling away from the nearest player deep inside his own twenty-five; black shirts and shorts in hopeful pursuit, and Phil Bennett, the player much criticised for not taking on the opposition at the time, gathers confidently, declining to kick for touch as everyone expected him to do. Instead he turns, ignores the touch line, and with all the panache of a ten-year-old playing 'internationals' with the kids next door in his own back garden, he begins to weave a delightful incisive pattern—a triple sidestep off his right foot— and in that moment there occur the three acts of deception if you like, and a great try is born, setting the tone for the truly admirable game which was to follow. It was also the true spirit of rugby football, the rare and memorable moment when a player is playing at a level other than the conscious, the unique moment when the game almost assumes an art form.

From *A Touch of Glory* by Alun Richards, published by Michael Joseph Ltd.

Rugby League

David Storey

THIS SPORTING LIFE

David Storey was a student at the Slade School of Fine Art, and is now a successful novelist and dramatist. His previous jobs included school-teaching and professional Rugby League. His novels won many leading awards, and two of his plays, including *The Changing Room*, the drama version of *This Sporting Life*, have been filmed.

The novel itself is a compelling study of the bitterness and disillusion of the professional Rugby world, and the slow death of hope in one who has always reacted against defeatism in others. This is a brutal world, one of exploitation and false hero-worship, raised sometimes to a higher level by the spirit of comradeship and mutual regard.

From THIS SPORTING LIFE

Maurice ran up like he'd done a thousand times before and kicked off. The six forwards ran down the field. I carried on a straight course, knowing I could give the impression of strong attack without having to do anything — the player gathering the ball would run obliquely to the centre of the field and pass to one of the half-backs.

This he did, giving a fast convenient pass to the little captain who'd scarcely collected the ball than he was nearly killed by a short-arm from Maurice coming up in anticipation. The man lay still, covered in mud, his short legs splayed over the grass. The ref went over with a warning glance at Maurice to see how dead the man was. 'That's the way, Maurice,' Frank said.

We made a scrum over the spot, the short piston limbs interlocking, then straining. A movement began across the field and young Arnie ran in with an ankle tap and the player crumbled. The ball rolled free and the boy scooped it up alertly with one hand and side-stepping started to run down the field. He found Frank with a long pass coming up laboriously in support. The great bulk of Frank, his lessened speed, drew the opposing forwards magnetically. They leapt wildly at his slow procession through them. Before he fell under their simultaneous attacks he flicked the ball expertly into the gap he'd deliberately created. Maurice, waiting in receipt, didn't hear the oppressive noise that came from Frank as he hit the ground; he took the ball one-handed and with short precise steps cut his way through to the fullback, and was almost on the line when the winger, coming across with a greater and more famous speed, knocked him over like a stalk.

The two teams shot into position in the thick din of excitement. Frank stood behind Maurice and took the ball as it came between the scrum-half's legs. I started running up from behind, Frank held the ball, then slipped it to me as I passed in full stride. I hit the wall of waiting men like a rock. For a second they yielded, drew together, and held. A dull pain shot from the top of my skull. I struggled into a position I knew would ease the impact and give me more chance with any excited fist. I heard through compressed ears the screams and groans of the crowd, almost the individual voices of agony, before I was flung down.

I rose with the same motion and played the ball. Young Arnie had it. I'd never realized how popular he was with the crowd. When, with an apparently casual blow, he was banged down, I was vaguely satisfied at his indiscretion. I took the ball as he played it and sent it to the centres. It passed straight to the super-protected wingman. He gathered cleanly and bustled up the field only to be shoved into touch. The crowd disapproved.

We folded down to the scrum, panting with the first breathlessness, steam rising from the straining 'backs. I saw the damp shape roll between my legs and Maurice snatched it up impatiently. With an extravagant dummy he shot by the still dazed captain and was caught by the winger. He kicked out, lashed out, contorted, and threw himself over the line.

The crowd screamed and surged like penned animals, like a suddenly disturbed pool. Whistles, bells, and trumpets crashed and soared on the animal roar. I ran to him, banged his back, and we walked back in pleased groups.

The full-back failed at goal. A slight breeze moved across the ground, spraying the drizzle. A spurt of vivid steam swirled over the pitch and drifted in slow ascent. I stared down at the bare patch of earth at my feet, soft and muddy. I bent down and touched it reassuringly, and as the flurry of rain changed direction looked up at the similarly worn patch at the centre. The ball wasn't there. A tiger was running across the spot just after kicking. I narrowed my eyes, and in the thick air, against the dark prominence of the cooling towers, saw the slim oval shape.

'Yours, Art!' Maurice shouted behind me. The wet leather smacked into my crooked arms and I twisted instinctively into the grip of the surrounding men. I fell comfortably and was pressed to the ground. I stopped to watch the ball move from hand to hand across the field.

'Come on, Arthur lad,' somebody shouted either behind me or from the crowd. I followed the ball mechanically, attached to it by an invisible string.

. . . . . .

The leather smacked into my outstretched hands. I ran straight at the man. 'Go on Art! Go on Art!' Maurice screamed behind me. I ran into him, over him. Trampled him and broke free into a gap. A pain thudded in my head in echo to my feet. An arm gripped my waist, slipped, caught again, and a fist sank into my neck. I carried him along. Then another caught me round the nose and eyes, the fingers explored for pain, forcing me to my knees. Arnie took the ball and with his boy's shout of triumph threw himself into the confusion of mud and men, his body searching, like a tentacle, for an opening. He ran ten yards to a scream from the crowd, then fell into the sea of limbs.

I was still kneeling, absorbed in an odd resigned feeling. My back teeth chattered as I pulled myself up, my hands shook with cold, and I despised myself for not feeling hate for the man who'd torn my nostril. I was used to everything now. Ten years of this, ten years of the crowd — I could make one mistake, one slight mistake only, and the whole tragedy of living, of being alive, would come into the crowd's throat and roar its pain like a maimed animal. The cry, the rage of the crowd echoed over and filled the valley — a shape came towards me in the gloom.

I glimpsed the fierce and brilliant whiteness of its eyes and clenched teeth through its mask of mud, flashing with a

Rugby League

useless hostility. It avoided my preparations to delay it, veering past out of reach. I put my foot out, and as the man stumbled took a swing with my fist. I missed, and fell down with a huge sound from the crowd. The man recovered and went on running. He ran between the posts. Frank picked me up, the mud covering my tears. Where's the bleeding fullback? I wanted to shout. But I could only stare unbelievingly at my legs which had betrayed me.

From *This Sporting Life* (pages 246-249) © David Storey, 1960, published by Penguin Books Ltd, 1962. Reprinted by permission of Penguin Books Ltd.

Golf

Pat Ward-Thomas

NINE HOLES WITH JACK NICKLAUS
THE AGONY OF THE FIRST HOLE AT ST ANDREWS
HOMAGE TO A PEERLESS GOLFER

Pat Ward-Thomas is one of the finest writers on the game of golf, and gave great pleasure to *Guardian* readers for many years. Recently he has written the official history of the Royal and Ancient Golf Club at St Andrews. He is most at home in his brilliant evocations of the game's personalities and of the truly great golf courses.

NINE HOLES WITH JACK NICKLAUS

At first thought the prospect of playing golf with Jack Nicklaus might seem forbidding, but I found it to be the very reverse. Down all the years of knowing and watching him, the opportunity of a game did not arise until last week in Florida, where Nicklaus now lives for the greater part of the year. After the Masters he went on a fishing trip and on his return said: "I must hit some balls before going to Dallas—would you like to play nine holes?" It did not take long to answer that one.

When I arrived at Lost Tree, the club across the way from his house, Nicklaus was on the practice tee thundering balls into the sunlit distance. He looked massively healthy in tennis shorts and white socks; members drifted by watching and chatting as he worked out problems with his driver, which was producing a rich variety of strokes, unlike the searing straightness of the irons.

For anyone who hits as hard as Nicklaus, and no one in history has ever hit harder, the minutest error in timing or in the angle of the club-face at impact, is likely to cause spectacular deviations. An observer will look for the conventional errors, like faulty rhythm, or moving ahead of the shot, but there was no visible trace of these things, especially the last, because he does stay so wonderfully behind the ball. I watched him with a tree as the background, and if anything his head moved slightly back rather than forward as he struck.

Stirring sight

There is no more stirring sight in golf than to see the long irons hit by a great and powerful golfer, like Nicklaus, Palmer, or Snead. Nicklaus was about to pass from the two iron to the three wood when I asked him to hit a few low with the one iron. To my mind this is the ultimate revelation of power, which no ordinary golfer can hope to achieve.

Nicklaus made no change in stance or, noticeably, in the position of his hands relative to the ball, which tore away, not rising more than eight feet until it had gone 100 yards or more, and finishing in the remote beyond. Some 25 yards in front of the tee were two seats with backs of wooden beams about an inch thick, and six inches apart. Jestingly he said: "Which gap would you like me to hit it through" and unleashed another terrible missile. The ball ripped through one of the slats, leaving a perfect semicircular hole, just as a bullet would have done, at the point of entry, splintering it vividly across the other side, and whistled on quite a long way. We shuddered at the thought of what the ball would have done to a human body.

When Nicklaus times the long irons perfectly, the sound of impact is like none other I have heard in its purity and sharpness. Later that afternoon I asked what he thought was the real source of his power. He patted a massive haunch and said, "I guess it's here" and, of course, he is right; the movement of weight at speed is the foundation not, as many believe, the strength of the hands. Strangely, Nicklaus's hands are on the small side and not particularly strong; the hardest squeeze of his grip is quite painless whereas the same is not true of Palmer. To ask him to grip your hand hard would be to invite a bone mincing. I once tried to snatch a club from his hands; it never moved and he said: "There's no way you can get that club."

When the practice was over we made for the first tee and the threshold of a memorable experience for me. "Go ahead," he said and to my relief I hit a solid shot, of perhaps 210 yards. Jack hit a towering push, dropped another ball and pulled it, and then uncorked a monumental shot down the fairway. As I got to my drive he said: "It's 200 to the middle of the green." The ball was in light rough. I took a three iron, and it finished just short of the green. A good shot I thought, but was soon sobered. From his last drive he needed only a firm wedge of perhaps 100 yards to the green. As Bobby Jones said once of Nicklaus, "He plays a game with which I am not familiar."

Playing with Nicklaus there is no temptation to press, because one knows the utter futility of it. We each hit two or three shots from every tee, and when both were reasonably good I realised as never before that his golf is of an entirely different dimension. One can sense this, of course, by simply watching, but to play beside it is another matter: to see a shot which would satisfy most golfers made to seem absolutely puny, is sobering and salutary to say the least.

Sound advice

As one would expect Nicklaus was charming to play with. Whenever I hit a bad shot he would make some brief and apposite comment. "Slower back for the first foot"—"You let go at the top" and so on. After a terrible bunker shot he patiently changed my method of playing these, showing why it is an advantage not to have the left shoulder higher than the right in the address. Although concerned with his own practice he always took time to watch my efforts, without being asked. This was the mark of rare courtesy.

Rarely have I enjoyed playing with anyone so much; rarely have I felt more at ease in the presence of a vastly superior golfer and there was the opportunity to admire without interruption and in private his method, strength, and talent. There were only the two of us and one caddie. Jack's second son, Stevie, aged 5, hit balls along with his little club, with the boundless energy and absorption of the very young, attacking them with great purpose and a fine eye.

Knowing that Nicklaus never pays idle compliments about anyone's golf I asked him whether he thought I was short for my build. He said: "I would expect you to hit the ball further with your swing, your right hand is not working hard enough," and showed how a change of weight distribution might help.

I realised yet again how observant he is, without appearing to be so, and hope continued to glow.

Nicklaus lives in a development of attractive one-storey houses around the course, on land between Lake Worth and the ocean, but the proximity of golf is not the attraction for him. He loves Florida for its climate and the easier tempo of life. "You have to have a change of pace. I've always tried to pace myself carefully—that's why I don't play too much on the winter tour, but maybe this year I haven't played quite enough."

Above all Florida offers fishing of a tremendous order in its scope and variety, and this has become something of a passion with him but not, as I feared, to the exclusion of golf. I went to Lost Tree prepared to ask him whether he intended to play less and how he visualised his future, and was there any thought of retirement in view, now that all worlds had been conquered. I asked none of these things: during the day we spent together the answers emerged.

Relaxation

That evening we sped over the lake and out into the ocean in his motor-boat, ably driven by Jackie junior, aged 7, and we saw the plot of land they had bought for a new house. The present one was thought too small for a growing family of three. We talked of how Barbara, his wife, was settling down in Florida after at first finding it lonesome, far away from friends and familiar surroundings in Columbus. Now Florida is regarded in a more permanent light and as Jack said: "I hope to be playing tournament golf for another five years or so—I love the competition." He had said earlier: "What I really like is to have to make a birdie and three pars on the last four holes to win."

Nicklaus is not one for the casual game; he would rather leave golf alone except for practice and tournaments. This is all part of his remarkable gift of detachment; he can easily arrange his life into different phases and not allow them to conflict. This has always been a problem for Palmer. As we bounded over the darkening ocean, and the warm twilight fell, I remarked that the four foot putts don't seem to matter out here, and he agreed. He seemed absolutely identified with the sea and the boat, standing easily as it bucked over the waves. Golf was in another world; it could never be an obsession with him and yet when he has to play his concentration and determination are absolute. Never has the old adage of a healthy mind in a healthy body been more true of

Golf

a golfer than it is of Nicklaus.

From the *Guardian*, 1 May 1968.

THE AGONY OF THE FIRST HOLE AT ST ANDREWS

The ultimate challenge of golf is the ability to produce one's best when it matters most and, except on rare team occasions, the mattering is entirely a personal affair. Long ago it was written: "Golf is not a wrestle with bogey; it is not a struggle with your mortal foe; it is a physiological, psychological, and moral fight with yourself."

This applies to every golfer, from the great man striving to win an Open championship to the humblest performer with his heart set on breaking 90. Whatever the degree of aptitude, technique, and experience, performance eventually depends on nerve; anyone can produce his shots on the practice ground, but the simplest stroke in a competition often strikes fear to the heart.

In all golf there can be no more revealing instance of this than the first hole on the Old Course at St Andrews. Few golfers are not familiar from personal experience, pictures, or hearsay with the hole's classic simplicity. The drive down the vast spread of greensward, unbroken by hazard of any kind, must be the most straightforward in the world, although this in itself can sometimes be a snare; but, except for a slice or hook of prodigious wildness, the ball is always in play. Then comes the problem.

Ahead lies the Swilcan Burn, from a distance just a faint dark line curving over the turf but, in fact, eight feet wide. It must be crossed if the round is to continue. The green, a generous, inviting expanse, lies immediately beyond the burn; the flag flutters enticingly; and apprehension mounts in the heart of the golfer — particularly those unaccustomed to precise keeping of their scores.

The approach can vary enormously, according to the wind and length of drive. Occasionally, it is prudent to play short and pitch over with the third, but even this is fraught with peril. The shot is delicate. One tries to nurse the ball close to the flag, perhaps 15 yards across the burn; it is early in the round and nerves are taut. How easy it is to quit on the shot so that the ball, feebly struck, plops gently into the clear waters or, jabbed with convulsive anxiety, races across the green and three putts invariably follow.

Golf

The awful psychology of the thing is that if the second shot goes into the burn, and the distance to the flag always looks shorter than it is, one is now playing four and trying desperately to avoid a six. There should be little difficulty; a simple pitch and run of 20 yards, no more; but there is the accursed burn at one's feet. Last year I faced this stroke. Deep in my heart I knew I was not going to make it.

The mind said: "Get the club back, swing smoothly through the ball, and don't look up"; but the club stopped with the sickening abruptness so familiar to the fluffer, and the ball just had sufficient impetus to roll over the edge from a range of six feet.

Months before playing in the Spring Medal last week, I resolved that, come what may, I would take enough club to carry the burn with plenty to spare. True contact with a 3 iron would have sufficed easily, but contact was minimal; the result, a perfect lay-up position for a short pitch, and what should have been at worst a five. Then the sabotaging forces, "the unconscious cerebrations," did their evil work; the ball rose in a feeble parabola and vanished.

I fashioned the traditional seven, as did one of my partners, a golfer long experienced at St Andrews, who hit a 5 iron plumb into the burn. He said later that he knew he should have taken a four but, as millions of golfers do, he made the deadly, false assumption that he would hit the shot perfectly, and from damp grass early in the morning.

All this may sound faintly ridiculous to those who have never played a Medal in agony at St Andrews, but I can assure them that it is not. The very next day, two eminent golfers of comparatively recent international vintage also opened with sevens. One chipped into the burn twice and tore up his card before he even crossed it, which must be some sort of record.

Although the burn is the obvious villain of the piece, the essence of the plot is the fear from within. If one played a Medal round every week over the Old Course, fear would diminish, even vanish, and the burn would seem to be the pleasant stream that it is — and not as one Australian golfer described it years ago, as the "— drine."

It all boils down to competitive practice; there is no conceivable substitute for anyone, Casper, Nicklaus, you or me.

From the *Guardian*, 15 May 1969.

Golf

HOMAGE TO A PEERLESS GOLFER

When Jones* came for the first World Amateur Team Championship he could only walk a little with the aid of sticks and he followed the golf in an electric cart. During the practice he moved about the course, reminiscently as might a man returning after many years to an old and beloved garden, doubtless he was recalling shots he had played and the moments of triumph and anxiety. He noticed any slight changes to the holes, including the little bunker that had trapped him behind the 11th green. Even the head greenkeeper was not aware that it had once been there. Throughout those days people would approach to pay their homage, the old ones who remembered and the young who wished they had known the beauty of his golf.

The championship was agonisingly close and one memory of the climax will never perish. William Hyndman was playing last for the United States, and as he stood on the 17th fairway in the fourth round it seemed certain that he had to finish with two fours, or even better, if his side were to survive. Jones had told his men that they must never play for the top level of the green, wise counsel in a team medal event, but the situation then was desperate. Hyndman looked across at Jones, sitting in his cart nearby, and indicated that he wanted to attempt the shot. Jones nodded agreement and Hyndman responded with as fine a stroke under severe pressure as St. Andrews had seen in many a year. His four iron shot bored through the deepening twilight to within five feet of the hole and his courage was rewarded when the putt fell for three.

In September that year the Town Clerk of St. Andrews had cabled Jones asking him to accept the Freedom of the City. The Ceremony in the Younger Graduation Hall of the University, was held on the second evening of the championship. It was the most emotional occasion that this writer has known in golf, as it probably was for the 1700 who filled the Hall. Had the building been larger two or three times as many people would have been there. The Provost of St. Andrews Robert Leonard welcomed Jones not only as a

---

*Robert Tyre ("Bobby") Jones, the only golfer to win the Open and Amateur Championships of Britain and America in the same year, "the impregnable quadrilateral".

Golf

distinguished golfer but as a man of outstanding character, courage and accomplishment well worthy to adorn the Roll of Honorary Burgesses. The last American thus honoured had been Doctor Benjamin Franklin almost two centuries earlier.

In making his reply Jones, who spoke as he wrote with an ease and grace given to precious few players of games, had no need of the notes he had prepared. He likened the Old Course to a 'wise old lady, whimsically tolerant of my impatience, but ready to reveal the secrets of her complex being, if I would only take the trouble to study and learn'.

How many golfers in their struggles to master the course must have realised the truth of this. Whether they could act upon it was another matter. Jones said that the more he studied the course the more he loved it, and that he came to appreciate that it was for him the most favourable meeting ground for an important contest. 'I felt that my knowledge of the course enabled me to play it with patience and restraint until she might exact her inevitable toll from my adversary, who might treat her with less respect and understanding.' Nicklaus might well echo these words.

Jones went on to speak of friendship. 'When I say, with due regard for the meaning of the word, that I am your friend, I have pledged to you the ultimate in loyalty and devotion. In some respects friendship may even transcend love, for in true friendship there is no place for jealousy. When, without more, I say that you are my friends, it is possible that I may be imposing upon you a greater burden than you are willing to assume. But when you have made me aware on many occasions that you have a kindly feeling toward me, and when you have honoured me by every means at your command, then when I call you my friend, I am at once affirming my high regard and affection for you and declaring my complete faith in you and trust in the sincerity of your expressions. And so, my fellow citizens of St. Andrews, it is with this appreciation of the full sense of the word that I salute you as my friends.'

Towards the end of his speech Jones said 'I could take out of my life everything except my experiences at St. Andrews and I would still have a rich full life'. It was small wonder that the people worshipped him. A few moments later his son helped him into his cart and as he and the Provost rode down the Hall together the people began to sing, 'Will Ye No Come Back Again'. It was a deeply moving moment with a deadly finality to it. Everyone knew that St. Andrews would never see him, or anyone like him, again. Herbert Warren Wind and I left the Hall together and some minutes passed before either of us could trust his voice.

From *The Royal and Ancient* by Pat Ward-Thomas, published by the Scottish Academic Press.

Peter Dobereiner

FADING INTO STARDOM
THE FLOWERING OF A FANTASY

Peter Dobereiner is Golf Correspondent to the *Guardian*, the *Observer*, *Golf World* and the American *Golf Digest*.

He is a lively, entertaining writer, always with an eye to the polemical, has a sharp sense of humour, and a predilection for the colourful phrase.

FADING INTO STARDOM

Henry Cotton once described the golf of one of his contemporaries in the following terms: 'He never hit a bad shot but somehow at the end of the day it always added up to 76.'

There are many golfers like that. Indeed, if we add an extra sprinkle of poetic licence to Cotton's remark, it could be said to apply to the majority of tournament professionals. They are the spear-carriers of pro golf, the strugglers who believe that they are on the way up and the strugglers who cannot accept that they are on the way down.

It is quite clear that anyone capable of scoring 76 off the back tees of a tournament course is a good enough striker to score 72 or, given a good day with the putter, a 69 or so. That last 5 per cent of improvement separates the stars from the chorus. Yet when you talk to those 76-scorers afterwards, and I hate to think how many times I have sat in locker rooms listening to hard luck stories, thay can always enumerate half a dozen instances of where they could have saved strokes.

Golf

Once in a blue moon I am impressed by the truth and honesty of these self-criticisms. One such confession was made by Peter Cowen at last year's Swiss Open. 'I missed two greens with a *six-iron*. A six-iron! Dammit, I can stand on the practice ground all day and hit my six-iron to the flag.' Why, I asked, did he miss those greens? 'Because in tournaments my grip tightens on the club. I've tried everything but nothing works. It still happens.'

Cowen retired from tournament golf. There was no more dedicated professional in British golf, few better strikers and none who worked harder at the game. I hope he makes a success of life as a club pro for he might well follow the example of Brian Waites; once he has security, once tournaments do not mean so much to him, he might show us his true capabilities.

The more usual explanation of a 76 is 'I missed five six-footers' or 'I chipped like an idiot and four times I didn't get it up and down.' Ask why and you get revealing, or concealing answers. 'Hell, even Jack Nicklaus misses a few greens now and then.' That is true enough, of course, but it does not answer the question. Too often the player pinpoints the missed putt or the feeble chip as the destructive shot, instead of pursuing his analysis to the reason why he was left with a six-foot putt or a chip from the fringe. The player then goes off to work on an imaginary fault, spending two hours over his six-footers when really it was his long putting which caused the problem; or chipping until darkness falls to cure what was actually a fault in his long irons.

It is a fact of golf that even the finest players make mistakes in every round. After a full year of operation of the American PGA's system of analysing every facet of golf we now have statistics which might, if we can only interpret them sensibly, isolate the real causes for good players taking 76 instead of 72.

The statistics are expressed in 10 tables and my own method of interpretation, after careful thought, was to throw four of the tables into the waste paper basket. The money list is valueless since it compares the man who has played 30 events with a player who has competed on only 10 occasions. The number of birdies, number of eagles, and par-breaking performances tell us nothing of much significance. Time has softened the memory but I still bang my head against the nearest wall when I recall the day from my lusty youth when I had five birdies and an eagle in a round of 85.

The method has to be to take the stroke averages (Lee

Golf

Trevino, 69.73; Tom Watson 69.95) and then to determine which skills contributed most to these results. The first, glaring conclusion which leaps from the statistics is that driving accuracy is much, much, much, much more important than driving length.

It goes without saying that every successful pro must give the ball a healthy wallop off the tee but within that broad generalisation there are big hitters (averaging about 270-275 yards), medium hitters (averaging 260-270) and those who cannot burst a grape (averaging less than 260 yards). Mike Reid is in the third category and yet he leads the American players in driving accuracy and he comes out with a scoring average of 70.78, making him sixth best player on the Tour. From the gorilla category, only one player from America's leading 10 long drivers (Nicklaus) figures in the top 10 averages, with 70.86, and he is not among the 10 most accurate drivers, although 13th place is not bad, specially as he sometimes drives into light rough on purpose.

The putting statistics confirm what we all know about putting, namely that it can make up for a multitude of sins (Watson, Jerry Pate and Ben Crenshaw are among the 10 best putters but not among the 50 straightest drivers). On the other hand good putting alone is not enough; the other seven top putters do not figure among the giants of American golf.

Saving par from bunkers is likewise a useful skill. Crenshaw's record of getting up and down from sand more often than not for ninth place in the table, plus his good putting, balances his wayward driving and subsequently moderate record in hitting greens in regulation figures (47th in the list). Nicklaus, on the other hand, heads the table for hitting greens in regulation. He does not have to play so many trap shots, which is just as well because he is not too good at them to judge by his absence from the list of the top 50 bunker players.

After driving accuracy, hitting greens in regulation figures correlates most closely to the stroke averages and it is clear (to me, anyway) that unless you have a freakishly good short game (i.e. Crenshaw) you have to hit those fairways off the tee. That is paramount if you are to score high in the department of hitting greens in regulation figures.

How should these findings be applied to the golf of youngsters who seek fame and fortune from the game? First, I suggest, they should assimilate the significance of accuracy being more important than length off the tee. Lusting after those extra few yards is the greatest single sin in pro golf. It is a natural ambition among boys to want to belt the cover off the ball but in nine cases out of 10, possibly more, it results in the development of a draw. And here we uncover the true meaning of those statistics. The leading 10 Americans in the stroke averages all habitually fade the ball off the tee, some of them (Andy Bean for example) having seen the light as reformed hookers. At last we have positive proof that all golf's blessings flow from a controlled fade off the tee, effectively making fairways twice as wide and making that all-important task of hitting the fairway twice as easy.

At this point I am aware of a pimply lout at the back of the class sniggering that you achieve the same result by aiming your drive down the right and hooking the ball back into the middle of the fairway. *And* you are left with a shorter approach.

That is the most damaging fallacy in pro golf. By and large, a faded drive sits down where it lands; the hooked drive pitches and runs — and serves you right if it runs under a bush. Go out, young man, and try to hook your way into the record books. You will find another 200 misguided youths on the tour trying to do the same thing. Either slug-hook your way into oblivion or ponder the wisdom of Tom Kite: 'I can usually contrive a way of finding the fairway with my natural fade.' Kite, let me tell you, had a stroke average of 70.96 last year. And, wait a minute while I rummage in the waste paper basket, he earned $150,000 on the US Tour alone.

From the *Observer*, 11 January 1981.

THE FLOWERING OF A FANTASY

Flying low along the Coachella Valley on the approach to Palm Springs, the mountain ranges of San Jacinto and Santa Rosa rise sheer on either side and you look down on flat desert. The only signs of life are the odd bundle of tumbleweed cartwheeling over the sand and State Highway 111 dividing the valley as if drawn by a ruler.

Gradually other lines appear, sectioning the desert into rectangles and then you see the first development as if a child with a paint box had been told to paint an octopus in one of the rectangles with lurid, incongruous emerald paint.

Of course! It is a golf course and the unpainted areas

Golf

between the tentacles are the sites for condominiums, apartments and villas as yet no more than an architect's impression in the developer's glossy brochure. More and more rectangles are painted in and by the time the traveller lands he can count 40 golf courses, including the private one of Mr Walter Annenberg, former Ambassador to the Court of St James, and probably the most exclusive course in the world.

My destination was the Vintage Club, which may be the game's ultimate extravaganza. They are coy about discussing costs but it is clear that your common or garden millionaire need not bother to apply for details of the Vintage development. If you have two million to spare for a holiday retreat then you might be considered.

My laundry having gone astray, I was less than my usual elegant self when I was challenged by the security guard at the gate of the Vintage Club. This being tournament week, when all kind of human dregs including newspapermen and professional golfers had to be tolerated, I was admitted but got the distinct feeling that it had been touch and go whether to have me arrested for vagrancy. When I asked in the pro's shop if they stocked cheap shirts I received the snotty response 'Nothing is cheap at the Vintage Club.'

I can well believe it after recoiling from the shock of the golf course. It is unlike anything I have ever seen, not even among the lavish creations of Japan. George and Tom Fazio were commissioned to build a course worthy of the spectacular concept of the development and the result is pure Salvador Dali. Whether you like it or not, you cannot help marvelling at what imagination can produce when released from the restraints of budget considerations. The central feature is a string of lakes connected by waterfalls, made of specially sculptured boulders which were shipped in from Arizona. (I swear on the heads of my children that I am not making this up).

The really innovative idea which the Fazios have introduced is the use of flowers. Everywhere in the course which is not needed for play, behind the tees, between holes and in the dead ground on short holes, they have planted flowers. Some are formal beds of the municipal parks department variety, some quite informal. There are rockeries the size of a cottage, one devoted to alpines and miniatures, another confined to varieties of cactus. One long mound has been planted with what looks like a variety of marigold, producing a hundred-yard splash of violent orange across the landscape.

The floral theme is used to stunning effect at the short

seventh where you drive from a platform tee on a rocky outcrop. The green is surrounded by flowers, in formal beds, a glorious profusion of wild flowers, and cacti in separate areas. It is like trying to hit your tee shot into the thumb hole of an artist's palette.

It is ironic that the Vintage Club should sponsor the Vintage Invitational Tournament for the players are nearly all veterans of those hard days during the Depression when they were trying to get a tournament circuit started. They did not play for money in the modern sense, because there was precious little money to play for, and the golfers like Jimmy Demaret often had to ride to the next tournament on freight trains. Sometimes they had to get away from their hotels out of a back window, and send a money order later when the putter turned hot and they made a few bucks.

But those ex-caddies and shop boys could play like hell and by their exploits they turned golf from a pastime for the privileged one per cent of the population into a national obsession claiming 20 million adherents. In a sense the Vintage Club is the culmination of their dedication to a game which offered them nothing but hard work and hardship.

From the *Observer*, 15 March 1981.

Alistair Cooke

JACKLIN WINS U.S. OPEN

Alistair Cooke won great fame for his B.B.C. documentary on America and its accompanying book, and his long-running *Letter from America* on radio. He wrote appraisals of film personalities, and found himself very much at home commenting on golf scenes and personalities in America.

JACKLIN WINS U.S. OPEN

New York, June 21

Tony Jacklin won the United States Open golf championship today by seven strokes from Dave Hill. Anyone over 50 must reel at the fantasy of the 26-year-old little English terrier with the sideburns and the cardigan of many colours, becoming the Open champion of the United States, which is to say, for all competitive purposes champion of the world.

For so long ago as the 1920s, the era of bobbed hair, Paul Whiteman, and bootleg booze, the Americans (in the immortal figure of Robert Tyre Jones) once and for all wrenched the mastery of the game from Britain. It has been 50 years precisely since an Englishman, Ted Ray, won the US Open. And it has been 17 years since anyone (who else but Ben Hogan?) led the field on the first day, and the second, and the third, and the last.

These were only two of the records that tumbled today on the Hazeltine course, in Chaska, Minnesota, on the final day of a US Open that is surely among the most contentious and dramatic of modern times and that is certainly the kookiest.

Bells tolled
The first dispatches out of Minnesota brought the dreadful

Golf

news that Jacklin had bogeyed both the seventh and eighth on the last round, and the bells began to toll for Tony. The litany was premature. One picture, they say, is worth a thousand words. And blessedly, the first picture that hit the television screens this evening was a beautiful running putt from 25 feet that rattled around the rim of the cup and dropped.

It was a birdie for Tony on the ninth and, we fervently hoped, the redeeming shot, the benzedrine injection that makes every disconsolate golfer think he is Walter Hagen, a carefree cavalier who cannot remember the last bad hole.

So it seemed, for on the tenth, after a pushed drive into the rough and a meticulous eight iron within six feet from the flag, he stroked another birdie and was now six under, five shots ahead of the sinister Dave Hill. He parred the eleventh. On the twelfth, after a fine drive he trotted up a hill, rooted the most immovable head in golf and swung a seven iron to the green. Yet again he left himself an agonising 5ft., and yet again the firm stroke had the old stars marvelling in the clubhouse.

Happy to par

Jacklin now went to the thirteenth and an unsatisfactory drive left him just off the far fringe of the green. He would be happy to par this one, and after a chip that curled 4 ft. beyond the hole, so he was.

On the fourteenth, where thick-foliage trees presented much trouble on the right, he took a safe iron and landed exactly where he should, down the middle left-hand side of the fairway. On the second shot he left himself 50ft. from the hole. There was total silence in Minnesota as he again anchored himself, took the shortest, squarest backswing and followed the true line to within a foot for a tap in.

Again a par on the 16th, again on the 17th, on the 18th a birdie. And so he had won. The roll call of honours—the 11th man in history to win both the United States and British Opens, the fourth man after Hagen, Jim Barnes, and Ben Hogan to lead the Open all the way, and only the second man to stay below par on all four rounds of the US Open. "He is," Dave Marr said, "a great guy and a fine golfer."

It began on Thursday with the gathering of the 130 top pros and a raspberry chorus of criticism about the innate unplayability of a long course.

It was, however, to Dave Hill, a young newcomer to the tour, to coin the $150 insult. Hill is a mop-headed youth with

Golf

granny glasses, an attractive geniality, and an unattractive air of Mr Know-all. "The man who designed this course," he said (none other than Robert Trent Jones) "had the blueprints upside down. If I had to play this course every day, I'd find another game."

The humiliation to the game's leading lights was so glaring that something drastic had to be done to persuade them to stay in Minnesota. If the qualifying score had been the usual 10 strokes off the leader, just 34 men would have been left in the game and 88 would have been benched. They called the cut at 153, a figure that could encourage us all to enter next year. Nicklaus, Palmer, and Player just squeaked into the company of their betters.

It was Saturday's play that gave the clue to Jacklin's quality and might also, I fear, presage his collapse. He began two strokes ahead of Hill and picked up another on the first hole from Hill's bogey. On the third, he left himself short by 8ft. for a birdie and made it. A nasty three-putts on the fifth was compensated on the eighth by another bogey from Hill. In other words, for the first nine, Hill was slipping and Jacklin was simply steady as he went.

On the back nine, Hill was mercilessly straight and had a 33 with three birdies. Why, then, should Jacklin's 35 be so comparatively inspiring? Because the little Englishman was so often nervy and imprecise on both his long and short approaches, and so monumentally nerveless on the greens. Time and again, his growing army of fans groaned when, from comfortable chips and easy pitches, he was four, five, and six feet short of the hole—in a major championship the murderous distances. Without exception, he rammed them home.

On the seventeenth, a beautiful and tortuous par 4 with a hilly dogleg, intruding trees, two lakes, and a high mound before the green, it seemed he had lost his command and broken his spirit. Against Hill's perfect drive, Jacklin hooked his into wild rough behind a soaring elm, and beyond it the lakes and the mound. Dave Marr passed on the whispered remark that there was no way out but to chip to safety and lose a stroke.

But the dogged little terrier trotted around the tree, squinnied at the lakes, went back and whammed an 8-iron high over the tree and the other hazards and stopped on the green, 30ft. from the hole. Warmed by the roaring ovation, he missed the birdie by a millimetre. It was a wonderful recall of Palmer in the great days.

From the *Guardian*, 22 June 1970.

Henry Longhurst

THE GREATEST TOURNAMENT IN THE WORLD

Henry Longhurst was Golf Correspondent of the *Sunday Times* for forty-five years, published thirteen books, and was a frequent broadcaster on the game in Britain and the United States. His weekly essay on golf in the *Sunday Times* was very widely read, with its strict economy of style and arrangement, its warm affection for the game, and his tart sense of humour. He was completely irreverent to those who took the game too seriously or over-emphasised its global importance. He loved the drama of great matches, but had most regard for the "characters" of the game, such as Walter Hagen, who took time "to smell the flowers".

Henry Longhurst took time to see a whole world of nature on golf courses, as he described in a radio broadcast.

He had a wonderful faculty for recreating the golfing scene, as we see here.

THE GREATEST TOURNAMENT IN THE WORLD

They made big, undulating greens and were, I believe, the first in America deliberately to make four different "pin positions"—a practice now common on nearly all new American courses of any consequence. This means that a shot good enough to stay near the flag leaves a comparatively simple putt for a birdie, while one that only finds the edge of the green leaves the player hard put to get down in two more. Furthermore, they try to keep the pace of the greens sufficiently fast so that a well-struck shot will hold, whereas one slightly skimmed, or "thinned," as they put it, will shoot over the back.

Golf

Four years after they started, Jones and Roberts decided to hold an invitational tournament, little knowing, I fancy, into what it was going to develop. They invited all the accepted masters of the game and almost from the beginning it became known as the Masters Tournament.

For a while they themselves decided who should be invited, but such was the immediate prestige of the tournament that a complicated system of qualification had to be devised, encompassing home and overseas players, professionals and amateurs. The sponsors nevertheless retain a power of discretion, and I suspect that anyone who started throwing clubs or tantrums in one year would not be invited the next, even if he were an Open champion.

"As far as I am concerned," Arnold Palmer has said, "there will never be another tournament like it." The winner is invested with a green blazer, almost the most distinguished emblem in American golf, and becomes a member of the Masters Club, which dines once a year, at the expense of the previous winner.

Most people, furthermore, seem to look upon the Masters as the best-run tournament in golf. "Any club that wants to see how a tournament should be conducted should dispatch a few emissaries to study the Masters," Gene Sarazen once commented. "The galleries are intelligently marshalled. The spectators as well as the golfers are treated as gentlemen. Jones will not tolerate the faintest suspicions of burlesque-show atmosphere . . . The flavour at the Masters reflects the personality of Robert Tyre Jones Jr., and Bob has always epitomized the best in golf."

It was during the second Masters Tournament in 1935 that Sarazen played what might almost be described as the most historic single shot in golf. As he walked towards his second shot at the 15th—then 485 yards long and rated par 5—a tremendous roar from the clubhouse signified that Craig Wood had finished with a birdie 3.

Consulting with his caddie Stovepipe—so called after the battered tall silk hat he always wore when caddying—Sarazen found that he needed four 3's, against a par of 5-3-4-4 to win.

He decided to take a 4-wood to get the ball up and over the intervening pond and "rode into the shot" with all his might. A moment later the spectators behind the green were jumping wildly in the air. He had holed out from 220 yards for 2! Poor Craig Wood. Sarazen tied and beat him in the playoff.

The Masters, regarded by so many as the greatest golf tournament in the world, has everything. A course which, as set for the players, is a tremendous test of nerve and skill; an organisation second to none; provision for the comfort and information of spectators that has grown steadily better every year; and an atmosphere all of its own, which has grown up perhaps through a combination of the qualities mentioned above. It is an event which is greater than any individual who participates in it.

The course is laid out among a combination of vast pine trees, shorter firs, and flowering trees and shrubs, including particularly azaleas. These are in full bloom for the tournament and the sight of the second part of the long 13th hole will live in my memory as long as I live. The hole is a dogleg to the left and a creek crosses the fairway and then proceeds up the left-hand side, turns with the dogleg and runs all alongside the second shot, finally turning again to cross directly in front of the green and wind away round the right-hand side of it. Meanwhile, along the left of the second shot the ground rises steeply and this bank is covered with the most magnificent orange, red and purple azaleas, all around the foot of pine trees which must be every inch of a hundred feet high. I spent much time there on my first visit, just gazing at it and committing it to memory.

We were fortunate too in the weather, the best they had ever had, I was told: four successive days of blazing sunshine that brought everything out, including the spectators, in gorgeous Technicolor. The grass, as green as could be, is an expensive combination of basic Bermuda, which provides an almost invisible brown and dormant undermatting to the vivid green rye, which at this time of year grows so fast that they have to mow it twice a day. Soon the winter rye will die and the course will be closed until October, when it is resown.

There is no rough on the Augusta National course, though of course there are plenty of trees and sand traps, especially round the greens. What makes it such a tremendous test is that from the Masters tees you have to be very long—the day of the "good little 'un" has long since gone in American golf—and you are then faced with the flag in any one of four pin positions on sharply sloping greens. On the final day the pins are put in really hideously difficult positions, sometimes only four yards from a slope rolling down into a trap, so that only a desperate man dares "have a go." It is this aspect more than any other, or so I felt, that means no one can fluke a win in the Masters. To play at these tiny targets knowing that you are playing them for many hundreds of thousands of dollars is a strain which anyone can understand.

From *Never On Weekdays* by Henry Longhurst, published by Cassell Ltd.

Stephen Potter
HANDICAP TYPES

Stephen Potter's concept of Gamesmanship originated in 1947. It was further developed in *The Complete Golf Gamesmanship* in 1968. The books themselves have become humorous classics, and the terms themselves, gamesmanship, lifemanship, one-upmanship, and the revitalised word "ploy", have passed into the language. The word "brinkmanship" was used by an American statesman as a direct borrowing from Potter's original idea.

HANDICAP TYPES

Parallel to, and independent of, Heart Handicaps is the fact that each *established* golfer acquires in time a fixed handicap. Handicap and player have coalesced.

It is not the characters of golfers which differ so much as the *character of their handicaps*.

Some people, unused to the pioneering discoveries of lifethought, are left breathless by such statements. But let he who says 'this is false' read through this first list of suggested handicap traits.

Take 24 as a start. This handicap for a woman is generally associated with an *ambitious nerviness* and a determination, long thwarted, to become 18. But in a man it has a suggestion of roundness and warmth. The 24 man is rarely a self deceiver. The 22 man on the other hand may be nigglingly mean and, however short with his woods, a very good putter. The unusual number 21 suggests an ex 24 who has recently won a toast rack. 20s are generally past their prime but are men of spirit. This they show by saying either that they have never had a day's illness in their lives or (in alternate weeks) that they are never really free from pain.

The character of 18 is split. There is a weak and colourless 18, with thin red hair perhaps, one whose skin never browns in the sun, a flaccid personality, an acid-drop sucker, never likely to get married, the sort of man who in the country looks as if he wishes he was in a town, and *vice versa*. But there is also a deep-voiced 18, a man who has recently given up football, a man of strength, who, though often off course, can, using only a spoon and number 8, slash his way round by sheer muscle.

More thin-blooded even than the 'weak' 18 is 17, with his unpleasant eyes a pale and watery blue. He finds it difficult to get opponents or is too mousey to ask for them. Old 16s are sound sensible people who may have been 7 before the war. Young ones, or more particularly young 15s, often emphasize that they are playing 'for fun' —i.e. that they are non-golfers—and don't like people who 'take the game too seriously'.* The longest handicap man to get the care-worn look of the really hooked or nearly hooked golfer is the 14. He spends time in the professional's shop looking at clubs, testing but never actually buying them. When he is about to address the ball he will be likely, because he has just read Gadman on *The Grip*, to take hold of the shaft with his left hand first, finger by finger, as if he were learning to play the recorder. There is a little secret something about him, which one may guess to be that he believes his handicap could just possibly be down to 12 after the next Committee Meeting. Any experienced gamesman can use this fact in the gamesplay.

Thirteens are rare: but 12s are all too common. This is the pleasant backwater of golf. All on a golden afternoon. Abandon ambition all ye who enter here. Twelves often chat during play. Nearly 15 per cent of the bar receipts come from 12s: and 12 is the average handicap of the Sunday four-ball quartet who have played together since 1946 or even '36. It is a rule that except for young players on the way down, 12s must never have their handicap altered until they reach the age of 85. They are not only difficult to beat in actual play; their gamesmanship is sometimes impregnable, though often primitive, (a common gambit, among old friends who play together regularly, is never to comment or change expression, even after a shot which is exceptionally good or particularly bad. Not in any situation do they say 'bad luck').

*In fact, people who are 'against taking the game too seriously' are really taking-the-game-seriously too seriously.

Golf

The biggest change comes with 11. At once this suggests a much more serious golfer, the highest handicap player to possess an inner fire. Cheeks pale and drawn, eyes intense and often too close together, 11 will keep to his handicap but only by constant effort and practice so unremitting that it may involve some slight physical deformity. Some 11s believe themselves to be under a curse. They seldom win the annual club knock-out.

The handicap of 10 is in strong contrast. It suggests a man more relaxed approaching the dignity of being Good at Games. Often he belongs to the 'really better than that' brigade, e.g. 10 may be really 8. A 9, on the other hand, is often a more genuine 11, under a special strain of trying to keep to single figures. In contrast again 8 and 7, often really 5, or at any rate on their way to better play, are distinguishable because 8 is not unhappy to remain 8 as he is beginning to enjoy collecting twinkling silver spoons and tinkling ash trays. Difficult to deal with in play, he is vulnerable in opposition to a superior trophyman. Eight is ambitious, exercises his grip fingers during working hours by suddenly clutching his umbrella, and practises the beginning of the swing with the right arm only, even if he is in Oporto, waiting for a taxi.

The 5 man, once he has achieved this splendidly low figure, is liable, unless he rapidly improves still further, to become fixed in the trap of his own virtuosity. Age stops the way to advance, pride stops re-adjustment during the eternal return to double figures. He continues to come to the Club but spends his playing time on the practice ground. How well I remember W.D.J.S. of Aldeburgh, who was often seen on the putting course, bent like a croquet hoop, or far away on the practice ground, east of the 14th. In the distance the sea darkened as the sun dropped low: but W.D. would be there, putting down yet another row of 40 golf balls, to hit them distances which were gradually to decrease, if only by a foot a year, with his No. 4 iron. Five, the highest handicap to suggest 'expert', he had attained. Five he was determined to be for ever. So he remains, one of the loneliest figures in the world of games, a ghost of the practice ground or wistfully following, at a distance, the gay careless pursuers of the monthly medal or the four-ball friendly.

The 4s and under belong to a special patrician class who *could* 'go round in level fours'. They are different, they are not us; though I myself have twice done level 4s: the first time was in 1936 at Chislehurst. This subjected me ever since to the heavy-handed gamesmanship play of 'that short course at Chislehurst', until years later I was level 4s at the really tough North Berwick.*

Three always sounds, by the mere precision of the number, as if it was really 3. The brilliant figure of 2 is again associated with the anti-parallelism of the absolute opposite. Two is either a dashing all-rounder occasionally playing cricket for Kent, or a dedicated monk-like character, who lives, like one of the *pujurats* of Istambul, in a stone cell, somewhere on the outskirts of the course. Scratch has to adopt the character of the schoolboy hero, not always easy, once the mid-thirties are passed, and plus 2 belongs to yet another world, the man from H.Q., umpiring matches in the Piccadilly Tournament, a man who must never be interrupted or spoken to on duty and even off it.†

From *The Complete Golf Gamesmanship* by Stephen Potter, published by William Heinemann Ltd.

---

* By a ploy which came to me on the spur of the moment. After breakfast at the Hotel I strolled onto the course with my clubs, took my driver on the first tee I came to (the 14th?), topped the drive, topped my iron, took an 8 to the edge of the green and holed my putt. For once I did the right thing. I walked in. 'I didn't finish the round,' I said—and remember that this exact wording is essential—'but when I came in I was level fours'.

† That the handicap itself suggests a character will be immediately clear if we think of figures of the pre-golf era. Everybody must agree that Julius Caesar was 11 down to the last detail of his *De Bello*, just as it is almost as clear that Pompey was a genuine 8 while Mark Antony, calling himself 6, was in fact much nearer to 16. Later on Mozart, passionately wanting to get down to single figures, was the bravest of 13s; Shakespeare would have played off the same handicap, but was too casual and absent-minded. Rubens would have given even more of the painting of his paintings to staff if he had indulged his obvious talents as a long handicap liable on occasion to do 80: Hazlitt's 3 would have been coldly passionate. Everybody would have been frightened of Dido, unpopular President of Sunningdale Women: but she would have been impossible to dislodge. Shelley and Baudelaire, Swinburne and Aubrey Beardsley, would be typical non-players. Although each in their different ways were lifemen, golf gamesmen were they never.

P.G.Wodehouse

RODNEY FAILS TO QUALIFY

P.G. Wodehouse was notable for the craftsmanship of his short stories, his inventiveness in the use of language, and the creativity of the idyllic, pastoral world that his superbly realized characters inhabit. He is a master of humour, and particularly so in his thirty-one golfing stories, compered by the Oldest Member (one of Wodehouse's most memorable characters). An example of this is in "Rodney Fails to Qualify", whose visual humour was brilliantly reproduced in a television adaptation.

From RODNEY FAILS TO QUALIFY

As a matter of fact, to be perfectly truthful, there was beginning already to germinate within her by this time a faint but definite regret that Rodney Spelvin had decided to accompany her on this qualifying round. It was sweet of him to bother to come, no doubt, but still there was something about Rodney that did not seem to blend with the holy atmosphere of a championship course. He was the one romance of her life and their souls were bound together for all eternity, but the fact remained that he did not appear to be able to keep still while she was making her shots, and his light humming, musical though it was, militated against accuracy on the green. He was humming now as she addressed her ball, and for an instant a spasm of irritation shot through her. She fought it down bravely and concentrated on her drive, and when the ball soared over the cross-bunker she forgot her annoyance. There is nothing so mellowing, so conducive to sweet and genial thoughts, as a real juicy one straight down the middle, and this was a pipterino.

"Nice work," said William Bates, approvingly.

Jane gave him a grateful smile and turned to Rodney. It

was his appreciation that she wanted. He was not a golfer, but even he must be able to see that her drive had been something out of the common.

Rodney Spelvin was standing with his back turned, gazing out over the rolling prospect, one hand shading his eyes.

"That vista there," said Rodney. "That calm, wooded hollow, bathed in the golden sunshine. It reminds me of the island-valley of Avilion——"

"Did you see my drive, Rodney?"

"——where falls not hail, or rain, or any snow, Nor ever wind blows loudly. Eh? Your drive? No, I didn't."

Again Jane Packard was aware of that faint, wistful regret. But this was swept away a few moments later in the ecstasy of a perfect iron-shot which plunked her ball nicely on to the green. The last time she had played this hole she had taken seven, for all round the plateau green are sinister sand-bunkers, each beckoning the ball into its hideous depths; and now she was on in two and life was very sweet. Putting was her strong point, so that there was no reason why she should not get a snappy four on one of the nastiest holes on the course. She glowed with a strange emotion as she took her putter, and as she bent over her ball the air seemed filled with soft music.

It was only when she started to concentrate on the line of her putt that this soft music began to bother her. Then, listening, she became aware that it proceeded from Rodney Spelvin. He was standing immediately behind her, humming an old French love-song. It was the sort of old French love-song to which she could have listened for hours in some scented garden under the young May moon, but on the green of the fourth at Mossy Heath it got right in amongst her nerve-centres.

"Rodney, *please*!"

"Eh?"

Jane found herself wishing that Rodney Spelvin would not say "Eh?" whenever she spoke to him.

"Do you mind not humming?" said Jane. "I want to putt."

"Putt on, child, putt on," said Rodney Spelvin indulgently. "I don't know what you mean, but, if it makes you happy to putt, putt to your heart's content."

Jane bent over her ball again. She had got the line now. She brought back her putter with infinite care.

"My God!" exclaimed Rodney Spelvin, going off like a bomb.

Jane's ball, sharply jabbed, shot past the hole and rolled on about three yards. She spun round in anguish. Rodney Spelvin was pointing at the horizon.

"*What* a bit of colour!" he cried. "Did you ever see such a bit of colour?"

"Oh, Rodney!" moaned Jane.

"Eh?"

Jane gulped and walked to her ball. Her fourth putt trickled into the hole.

"Did you win?" said Rodney Spelvin, amiably.

Jane walked to the fifth tee in silence.

The fifth and sixth holes at Mossy Heath are long, but they offer little trouble to those who are able to keep straight. It is as if the architect of the course had relaxed over these two in order to ensure that his malignant mind should be at its freshest and keenest when he came to design the pestilential seventh. This seventh, as you may remember, is the hole at which Sandy McHoots, then Open Champion, took an eleven on an important occasion. It is a short hole, and a full mashie will take you nicely on to the green, provided you can carry the river that frolics just beyond the tee and seems to plead with you to throw it a ball to play with. Once on the green, however, the problem is to stay there. The green itself is about the size of a drawing-room carpet, and in the summer, when the ground is hard, a ball that has not the maximum of back-spin is apt to touch lightly and bound off into the river beyond; for this is an island green, where the stream bends like a serpent. I refresh your memory with these facts in order that you may appreciate to the full what Jane Packard was up against.

The woman with whom Jane was partnered had the honour, and drove a nice high ball which fell into one of the bunkers to the left. She was a silent, patient-looking woman, and she seemed to regard this as perfectly satisfactory. She withdrew from the tee and made way for Jane.

"Nice work!" said William Bates, a moment later. For Jane's ball, soaring in a perfect arc, was dropping, it seemed on the very pin.

"Oh, Rodney, look!" cried Jane.

"Eh?" said Rodney Spelvin.

His remark was drowned in a passionate squeal of agony from his betrothed. The most poignant of all tragedies had occurred. The ball, touching the green, leaped like a young lamb, scuttled past the pin, and took a running dive over the cliff.

Golf

There was a silence. Jane's partner, who was seated on the bench by the sand-box reading a pocket edition in limp leather of Vardon's *What Every Young Golfer Should Know*, with which she had been refreshing herself at odd moments all through the round, had not observed the incident. William Bates, with the tact of a true golfer, refrained from comment. Jane was herself swallowing painfully. It was left to Rodney Spelvin to break the silence.

"Good!" he said.

Jane Packard turned like a stepped-on worm.

"What do you mean, good?"

"You hit your ball farther than she did."

"I sent it into the river," said Jane, in a low, toneless voice.

"Capital!" said Rodney Spelvin, delicately masking a yawn with two fingers of his shapely right hand. "Capital! Capital!"

Her face contorted with pain, Jane put down another ball.

"Playing three," she said.

The student of Vardon marked the place in her book with her thumb, looked up, nodded, and resumed her reading.

"Nice w——" began William Bates, as the ball soared off the tee, and checked himself abruptly. Already he could see that the unfortunate girl had put too little beef into it. The ball was falling, falling. It fell. A crystal fountain flashed up towards the sun. The ball lay floating on the bosom of the stream, only some few feet short of the island. But, as has been well pointed out, that little less and how far away!

"Playing five!" said Jane, between her teeth.

"What," inquired Rodney Spelvin, chattily, lighting a cigarette, "is the record break?"

"Playing *five*," said Jane, with a dreadful calm, and gripped her mashie.

"Half a second," said William Bates, suddenly. "I say, I believe you could play that last one from where it floats. A good crisp slosh with a niblick would put you on, and you'd be there in four, with a chance for a five. Worth trying, what? I mean, no sense in dropping strokes unless you have to."

Jane's eyes were gleaming. She threw William a look of infinite gratitude.

"Why, I believe I could!"

"Worth having a dash."

"There's a boat down there!"

"I could row," said William.

"I could stand in the middle and slosh," cried Jane.

Golf

"And what's-his-name——*that*," said William, jerking his head in the direction of Rodney Spelvin, who was strolling up and down behind the tee, humming a gay Venetian barcarolle, "could steer."

"William," said Jane, fervently, "you're a darling."

"Oh, I don't know," said William, modestly.

"There's no one like you in the world. Rodney!"

"Eh?" said Rodney Spelvin.

"We're going out in that boat. I want you to steer."

Rodney Spelvin's face showed appreciation of the change of programme. Golf bored him, but what could be nicer than a gentle row in a boat.

"Capital!" he said. "Capital! Capital!"

There was a dreamy look in Rodney Spelvin's eyes as he leaned back with the tiller-ropes in his hands. This was just his idea of the proper way of passing a summer afternoon. Drifting lazily over the silver surface of the stream. His eyes closed. He began to murmur softly:

"All today the slow sleek ripples hardly bear up shoreward,
Charged with sighs more light than laughter, faint and fair,
Like a woodland lake's weak wavelets lightly lingering
    forward,
Soft and listless as the—— Here! Hi!"

For at this moment the silver surface of the stream was violently split by a vigorously-wielded niblick, the boat lurched drunkenly, and over his Panama-hatted head and down his grey-flannelled torso there descended a cascade of water.

"Here! Hi!" cried Rodney Spelvin.

He cleared his eyes and gazed reproachfully. Jane and William Bates were peering into the depths.

"I missed it," said Jane.

"There she spouts!" said William pointing. "Ready?"

Jane raised her niblick.

"Here! Hi!" bleated Rodney Spelvin, as a second cascade poured damply over him.

He shook the drops off his face, and perceived that Jane was regarding him with hostility.

"I do wish you wouldn't talk just as I am swinging," she said, pettishly. "Now you've made me miss it again! If you can't keep quiet, I wish you wouldn't insist on coming round with one. Can you see it, William?"

"There she blows," said William Bates.

"Here! You aren't going to do it *again*, are you?" cried Rodney Spelvin.

Jane bared her teeth.

"I'm going to get that ball on to the green if I have to stay here all night," she said.

Rodney Spelvin looked at her and shuddered. Was this the quiet, dreamy girl he had loved? This Mænad? Her hair was lying in damp wisps about her face, her eyes were shining with an unearthly light.

"No, but really——" he faltered.

Jane stamped her foot.

"What *are* you making all this fuss about, Rodney?" she snapped. "Where is it, William?"

"There she dips," said William. "Playing six."

"Playing six."

"Let her go," said William.

"Let her go it is!" said Jane.

A perfect understanding seemed to prevail between these two.

Splash!

The woman on the bank looked up from her Vardon as Rodney Spelvin's agonized scream rent the air. She saw a boat upon the water, a man rowing the boat, another man, hatless, gesticulating in the stern, a girl beating the water with a niblick. She nodded placidly and understandingly. A niblick was the club she would have used in such circumstances. Everything appeared to her entirely regular and orthodox. She resumed her book.

Splash!

"Playing fifteen," said Jane.

"Fifteen is right," said William Bates.

Splash! Splash! Splash!

"Playing forty-four."

"Forty-four is correct."

Splash! Splash! Splash! Splash!

"Eighty-three?" said Jane, brushing the hair out of her eyes.

"No. Only eighty-two," said William Bates.

"Where is it?"

"There she drifts."

A dripping figure rose violently in the stern of the boat, spouting water like a public fountain. For what seemed to him like an eternity Rodney Spelvin had ducked and spluttered and writhed, and now it came to him abruptly that he was through. He bounded from his seat, and at the same time Jane swung with all the force of her supple body. There was a splash beside which all the other splashes had been as

Golf

nothing. The boat overturned and went drifting away. Three bodies plunged into the stream. Three heads emerged from the water.

The woman on the bank looked absently in their direction. Then she resumed her book.

"It's all right," said William Bates, contentedly. "We're in our depth."

"My bag!" cried Jane. "My bag of clubs!"

"Must have sunk," said William.

"Rodney," said Jane, "my bag of clubs is at the bottom somewhere. Dive under and swim about and try to find it."

"It's bound to be around somewhere," said William Bates encouragingly.

Rodney Spelvin drew himself up to his full height. It was not an easy thing to do, for it was muddy where he stood, but he did it.

"Damn your bag of clubs!" he bellowed, lost to all shame. "I'm going home!"

With painful steps, tripping from time to time and vanishing beneath the surface, he sloshed to the shore. For a moment he paused on the bank, silhouetted against the summer sky, then he was gone.

Jane Packard and William Bates watched him go with amazed eyes.

"I never would have dreamed," said Jane, dazedly, "that he was that sort of man."

"A bad lot," said William Bates.

"The sort of man to be upset by the merest trifle!"

"Must have a naturally bad disposition," said William Bates.

"Why, if a little thing like this could make him so rude and brutal and horrid, it wouldn't be *safe* to marry him!"

"Taking a big chance," agreed William Bates. "Sort of fellow who would water the cat's milk and kick the baby in the face." He took a deep breath and disappeared. "Here are your clubs, old girl," he said, coming to the surface again. "Only wanted a bit of looking for."

"Oh, William," said Jane, "you are the most wonderful man on earth!"

"Would you go as far as that?" said William.

"I was mad, mad, ever to get engaged to that brute!"

"Now there," said William Bates, removing an eel from his left breast-pocket, "I'm absolutely with you. Thought so all along, but didn't like to say so. What I mean is, a girl like you—keen on golf and all that sort of thing—ought to marry a chap like me—keen on golf and everything of that description."

"William," cried Jane, passionately, detaching a newt from her right ear, "I will!"

"Silly nonsense, when you come right down to it, your marrying a fellow who doesn't play golf. Nothing in it."

"I'll break off the engagement the moment I get home."

"You couldn't make a sounder move, old girl."

"William!"

"Jane!"

The woman on the bank, glancing up as she turned a page, saw a man and a girl embracing, up to their waists in water. It seemed to have nothing to do with her. She resumed her book.

Jane looked lovingly into William's eyes.

"William," she said, "I think I have loved you all my life."

"Jane," said William, "I'm dashed sure I've loved *you* all *my* life. Meant to tell you so a dozen times, but something always seemed to come up."

"William," said Jane, "you're an angel and a darling. Where's the ball?"

"There she pops."

"Playing eighty-four?"

"Eighty-four it is," said William. "Slow back, keep your eye on the ball, and don't press."

The woman on the bank began Chapter Twenty-five.

From "Rodney Fails to Qualify" from *The Golf Omnibus* by P.G. Wodehouse. Reprinted by courtesy of the Estate of P.G. Wodehouse and the Hutchinson Group Ltd.

Bernard Darwin

THE LINKS OF EIDERDOWN

Bernard Darwin, a truly great prose writer, was Golf Correspondent of the *Times* from 1907 until 1953. He also wrote for *Country Life*, and was the author of over twenty books.

His love of the game, his humour, and rich powers of expression are always features of his incomparably urbane essays.

In the essay, "The Links of Eiderdown" (1934), Darwin maintains that there "are few pleasanter things than a day in bed", so long as we shall soon be quite well. Callers can be ignored, and from our "halfway house between sleep and waking" we can "come to ourselves ready for another go of *David Copperfield*". There is just one thing to disturb all this . . .

From THE LINKS OF EIDERDOWN

Only one thing disturbed my serenity. In my warped mind's eye I continually saw golf holes designed on the 'land of counterpane' before me. It is not an uninteresting one, this links of eiderdown, and is laid out on what an ingratiating prospectus would call fine, undulating country. Moreover, by undulating himself in bed the patient can in a moment change the contour of his course. In the ordinary way there is a broad hog's-back ridge extending down the middle of the course. It is doubtless possible to use it in several ways, but I always saw a long plain hole running nearly the whole length of it, slightly downhill with a fall to perdition on either side for the slicer or hooker. It seemed to me, if I remembered the number aright, rather like the 13th hole at Liphook. There were no bunkers on it of any kind; no 'lighthouses', as the more ferocious of architects scornfully term them, to guide the eye of the tiger and make superfluously wretched the rabbit's life; nothing but a wide expanse on which it would clearly be very difficult to judge distance.

When my eyes dropped to either side of this ridge I felt that I was in another country. Was I at Formby or Birkdale, or perhaps at the 6th hole at Prince's, Sandwich? Here, at any rate, was one of the holes that run along a narrow valley with slopes on either hand — on one side, to be precise, the patient's leg, and on the other the outside edge of the eider-down. I have always had rather a romantic affection for such holes. I have heard with pain from those same 'highbrow' architects that they are not really good holes, because the mere fact of the banks (which will kick the ball back to the middle) give the player confidence, whereas the architect's duty is to make him hesitating and uncomfortable. I began to think that these irritating views were right; the valley might be narrow, but I felt as if I could drive straight down it, whereas when I looked at the ridge I did not feel nearly so happy.

There were other holes on the course, but they were hardly so satisfactory. There was, to be sure, a big, blind tee shot, to a one-shot hole as I imagined it, over a comparatively noble hill, made by my toes, but somehow it lacked subtlety; and when by a swift piece of engineering I moved the hill to see what the green was like on the far side, it proved flat and featureless. By separating and then adroitly manipulating my two sets of toes it was possible to make a crater green, with visions of the ball running round the side wall and back wall to lie dead at least for an unmerited three. That brought back sentimental memories. I knew a beloved course once that had three such greens running, and many years ago I had three threes running there and won a medal thereby. Still, the sweetness of such threes has a cloying quality. No doubt it is all for the best in the most testing of all possible worlds that there should be no more greens like that nowadays.

To roll over on my side had a disappointing effect on the links. In fact it was obviously not a links any longer, but a mere course: one of those courses on downland which I have the misfortune to dislike, with long, steep slopes, equally tedious to play up or down, and too often adorned with 'gun-platform' greens. When tea came, however, the course took on a new aspect, for the tea-tray was on a bed table and the bed table had four legs. The course was now one cut out of a wood, on which the architect had wisely allowed a solitary sentinel tree or two to remain standing in the middle of the fairway. The valley holes instantly became far more interesting, for each of them had one tree, acting in some sort as a Principal's Nose, for the tee shot, and another, like that capital tree at the first hole at Frilford, bang in front of the green. I spent some time trying to resolve on which side of those trees to go. At one hole it seemed best to try the right-hand line, because if I went to the left I might hook on to the floor, which was clearly out of bounds. At the other hole an exactly converse policy was indicated, but even with the banks to help me the shot was far from easy.

Now I am, as Mr Littimer would say, 'tolerably well' again, and *David Copperfield* is finished. I have no reasonable pretext for not getting up for breakfast, and indeed it is rumoured that there are to be sausages tomorrow morning. The links of eiderdown are fast becoming of the fabric of a dream. I have tried to fix the holes before they elude the frantic clutches of memory and fade away into one another.

From "The Links of Eiderdown" by Bernard Darwin, from *Mostly Golf*, edited by Peter Ryde, published by Adam and Charles Black.

Lawn Tennis

David Gray

THE SPRINGTIME OF A GREAT TALENT

David Gray's reports on Lawn Tennis for the *Guardian* were always highlights of the sports' pages for those who appreciated his enthusiasm for the game and his powers of description. Since then he has taken a key administrative post in world tennis.

His reports on the breakthrough of Evonne Goolagong (Mrs Cawley), and her final success in the Wimbledon Ladies' Championship give a powerful evocation of this buoyant, talented player.

THE SPRINGTIME OF A GREAT TALENT

In a little more than an hour the whole world of women's lawn tennis was turned upside down at Wimbledon yesterday. Margaret Court, the top seed, the reigning champion, and last year the second woman in the history of the game to achieve the grand slam of the four major singles titles, fell by 6-4, 6-1 to Evonne Goolagong, her 19-year-old challenger, playing in only her second Wimbledon.

It was not only the result which was a surprise, although Miss Goolagong had beaten the senior Australian at Melbourne earlier in the year and had run her close in the national championships at Sydney, but the manner in which it was accomplished. The margin of victory was the widest since Althea Gibson beat Darlene Hard in the 1957 final and she is the youngest champion since Karen Susman in 1962. It is also true to say that she is the most exciting champion Wimbledon has known since Maria Bueno, another 19-year-old, who won in 1959.

She lost only one set—a bad beginning to her fourth round match against Lesley Hunt on the windy first Saturday—on her way to the title and in her splendid second week, she beat Nancy Gunter at a cost of five games, Billie-Jean King 6-4, 6-4, and then ended with a brilliant flourish of graceful courage against Mrs Court. The tougher the matches, the better she plays. Her nerves held. While more experienced players struggled for accuracy, took deep breaths and tried to conquer their inhibitions, she continued her serene progress through the tournament.

Roughly translated "Goolagong" means "tall trees and cool water" in the Aboriginal language. That summons up the right kind of image. Calmly, naturally, she flowed through this tournament. Everything came evenly to her. She was able to make comments like: "I never have a set plan when I play anyone. I just go and play how I feel." The girl from Barellen, not far from the Murrumbidgee River, on her second journey out of Australia, cut down the old aristocracy of the women's game quietly, shyly, and effectively.

Scarcely a squeak has been heard from the "Women's Lib" (was that winter tour of the United States too long and too taxing for those who took part in it?). Everyone has been busily looking at Miss Goolagong and wondering whether she could go on hitting beautiful shots in risky situations. Instinctive tennis is the easiest of all tennis to appreciate. Her attack was simple and direct. Nor did she heap on herself the burden of overmuch expectation. She did not expect to win the title this year.

Vic Edwards, her coach, had always said she would not reach her competitive peak until 1974, but she said yesterday that when she beat Mrs King she thought to herself: "I have won the semis, so I may as well try for the final." She enjoyed yesterday's match, waiting to go on to the court made her feel nervous, but once the match began she felt at home on the Centre Court. "I am pretty used to playing there now." So she should be. She has more friends there than anyone else except, perhaps, Rosewall, Gonzales, and Christine Janes.

She was the first winner they had backed. And, oddly, once she had moved ahead in the second set we had the oddity of hearing sympathetic applause for Mrs Court—a sound which hadn't been heard since Billie-Jean King beat her in the first match in 1961 when the Australian girl had been seeded number one. Mrs Court had steam-rollered her way through, losing a set only to Judy Dalton and otherwise looking as formidably efficient as ever. She had won seven successive matches against Miss Goolagong and there was no particular reason to think the pattern would be changed yesterday—except that Miss Goolagong was responding to pressure in a way which was quite different from any other player in the women's events.

The tide seemed to be flowing for her. At deuce she would go for her shot in a way nobody else did. Mrs Court can't have underestimated the task. She was up against an athletic player with great speed and the power to hit clean, fierce shots with absolutely nothing to lose. In a way, it was the same situation as the final between Darlene Hard and Maria Bueno in 1959. Mrs Court is a considerably better player than Miss Hard ever was but she, too, found herself bewildered and outwitted by the sheer confident force of natural ability.

The beginning was daunting. Mrs Court served her way to 40-15 in the first game, and then was beaten by a couple of forehands. The capture of that game was followed by a surge of aggression from the younger player. She was gentle between points, smiling shyly with pleasure whenever anything went right and sharply resolute when she had to hit the ball. That is the way Wimbledon likes its players, not snarling with fury all the time but somehow managing to walk the awkward tightrope between toughness and femininity. Mr Tinling had dressed Miss Goolagong perfectly for this role.

She went to 4-0 and then at last Mrs Court began to move with a little of her usual majesty. She won the next three games and reached 40-15 on Miss Goolagong's service for four-all. Suddenly Miss Goolagong, whose service was always a springboard for attack when it worked properly, counter-attacked. A couple of forehand volleys, a rally in which she was lucky to get away with a dropshot to Mrs Court's backhand, and that most deadly of all volleys, a couple mishit, carried her to 5-3. Both held service after this but Miss Goolagong's service game carried her to the set.

The net cord helped her when Mrs Court held a game point for five-all but there was nothing lucky about the net cord and the smash which finished that crucial game. They were positive strokes, the sort that leave even champions without reply.

In the second set Mrs Court won the first game and no other. Miss Goolagong began to take more and more risks and more and more often they succeeded. The champion tried hitting hard and soft, mixing slices and spins, but nothing could save her.

"I wasn't moving well or concentrating at all. She was relaxed and went for everything. I could not find any rhythm or depth in my shots. I felt as though I was on a football field rather than a tennis court. If I had got back into the match in that eighth game of the first set, it might have changed everything."

She had game points in plenty but always she was frustrated. In the end she became almost statuesque. Miss Goolagong kept making her bend to nasty little low volleys near the net and she could not get them over. She kept on plugging away to the end. After all, she had won matches from situations like a set and 1-5 down in the past—as Winnie Shaw will remember. But in the end she put a backhand volley into the net and sentenced herself to losing the title by serving a double fault. She had won it three times, but she has never managed to win it for two years in succession. Immediately the centre court erupted.

When Miss Goolagong stood at the umpire's chair at the end waiting for Princess Alexandra to present her with the championship shield, she looked over where Vic Edwards and his wife were sitting and grinned. We almost felt we had watched a piece of brilliant impudence. The new queen had caught everyone off-guard and nipped away with the crown. She will wear it modestly. It is good to see a player who manages to win great tournaments and still feels tennis is a joke that has just begun.

From the *Guardian*, 3 July 1971.

Rex Bellamy

THE GREATEST TENNIS SHOW ON EARTH

Rex Bellamy, Lawn Tennis Correspondent of the *Times*, has written about the game in all the phases of its quite dramatic development throughout the world. In his book, *The Tennis Set*, he gives a graphic account of Wimbledon, the world's most prestigious tournament.

THE GREATEST TENNIS SHOW ON EARTH

The Wimbledon championships are the best shop window for tennis. They are also one of its worst. They are the best because of the splendour of the setting and the sense of tradition that casts a glow within it; because of the size and nature of the crowds; because of the huge and eclectic entry; because of the slick organization; and because the courts (and indeed, the grounds as a whole) are smartly maintained. They are among the worst because the courts are grass, which does not induce the players to paint the game in its loveliest colours. In the select gallery of great tournaments, Wimbledon is a picture of thrilling, awesome beauty—with a flaw in its central subject.

This is not to suggest that its grass courts should be torn up and replaced by something better. Variety is essential. Uniform playing conditions would breed a uniform playing style, and that would strip the game of the joyous contrast between slow-court and fast-court specialists. But in terms of variety, an accident of history gave Wimbledon the worst of the deal. In every respect except one, its supremacy is unchallenged. But we see better tennis on clay and on at least two of the new synthetic courts.

The faster surfaces are losing favour. Grass is a minority surface that seems slightly eccentric—and is coming to be regarded as an anachronism—in the context of the international circuit.

Wimbledon produces the best tennis only within the technical and tactical restrictions grass imposes. The courts tend to be peopled by big men with muscles and small men with problems. Rallies are short. Two strokes, the service and volley, are often tediously dominant. All is split-second timing. In its own way, this powerful game can be laudable, even exciting. But it can also be a crashing, bashing bore. Grass courts exalt strength and reflexes: both admirable qualities, but not to the exclusion of the more imaginative tactical pleasures of the game. In tennis, as in painting and music and drama, the fact that a task is technically difficult does not necessarily make it good entertainment.

In reducing a richly coloured game to stark black and white, Wimbledon does not even offer the players their most rigorous test of all-round ability. From a physical point of view it is not the toughest tournament to win.

Nor is it the richest. And in 1972 it can no longer pretend to its former status as an unofficial world championship. Because in 1971 the International Lawn Tennis Federation took the daft and damaging decision to exclude World Championship Tennis (an independent organization with more than 30 leading men under contract) from all events that recognize the authority of the ILTF's constituent national associations. In such a situation, Wimbledon was bound to suffer.

To put the worst interpretation on all these factors, it is possible to foresee a time when Wimbledon will no longer draw sell-out crowds and inspire massive international publicity. Because the sporting public have only a limited appetite for a sub-standard dish, however well served.

It is not a habit of mine to take such a pessimistic line. I have done so now in order to lend perspective to our view of Wimbledon, and to remind us that we should not take it for granted. It has always been the supreme festival of world tennis. But it need not necessarily remain so. Its soundest insurance for the future is the admirably forward-looking All England Club, which has acquired the habit of success and is unlikely to be satisfied with anything less.

Wimbledon is a sporting and social occasion that makes

news all over the world. It is a time of reunion for players of the present and the past. It brings together teenage enthusiasts and grizzled connoisseurs. It is an annual meeting of world tennis held in a pervading air of tension. The tradition of the tournament inspires everyone's endeavours. The mystique of royal patronage is itself a bond with an old glory that hangs like a sunlit mist over those green lawns in the land where tennis was born. Ghosts flit about the courts. Because in the mind's eye the giants of the past are still with us: indeed, many are there in the flesh.

The graceful grounds give the international game a beautifully designed spiritual home. The setting is lovely, with hydrangeas brightly patterned against a green backcloth of grass, trees, hedges, and those famous ivy-clad walls. The year-round labours of the staff keep the place in perfect condition: or as near perfection as it is humanly possible to get.

Wimbledon can be old-fashioned in its bland urbanity, yet is modern in the hard-headed professionalism of its players and administrators. Months of preparation precede the championships. On the first day the staff is swollen to the dimensions of a small army, and the organization slips back into gear as if it had never been in neutral. The work is painstaking. No detail is forgotten.

The players are cared for with such consideration that they have nothing to worry about except their tennis. They even have shining, chauffeur-driven limousines to carry them to and from the grounds. They must feel like gods and goddesses as the polished procession of black cars purrs slowly along the crowded promenade. The players feel cosseted, important, eager to do their best.

To win Wimbledon a player must be at a physical and mental peak, with a hot game and a cold brain. Because Wimbledon is an intimidating test of nerve and confidence and maturity, of the specific skills grass courts demand, and of strength and fitness. "The guy who is in the best physical shape has got a hell of an advantage in the second week", says Arthur Ashe.

But when a player has a Wimbledon title among his references, his reputation is secure. This, above all others, is the tournament they want to win—because of the character and prestige of the event itself, not because of the prize money or off-court benefits (a Wimbledon champion is prime bait for manufacturers who want a "name" to endorse their products).

Lawn Tennis

The force that knits all these separate strands together and makes Wimbledon such a vivid occasion is the swarming enthusiasm of the sophisticated crowds who pack the grounds every day. For many of these people, as for the players, merely to be at Wimbledon is fulfilment in itself. Some spend hours queuing in tunnels beside the courts of their preference, and do not look discontented. Others cluster on the promenade, watching the electric scoreboards and echoing the roars from the centre court and court one.

For tennis, Wimbledon is the greatest show on earth. There is a tingling flavour in the air that enters the bloodstream and quickens the pulse rate. Going through the gates on the first day is a moment to catch the hearts of starry-eyed young players who have not been there before. One said it was like going into a cathedral, and that was an apt comparison: because to the tennis sect, Wimbledon is sacred ground.

From *The Tennis Set* by Rex Bellamy, published by Cassell Ltd.

Max Robertson

MAUREEN CONNOLLY

Max Robertson has been described as "the voice of tennis on B.B.C. radio since the war". In his elegant and graphic style he has been able in his broadcasts to capture the excitement, thrills and tension of the greatest matches that have occurred on the Centre Court. He is an authority on tennis history and has written the authentic history of Wimbledon, *the Centre Court of the Game*. He became known to a wider audience as Chairman of the B.B.C. television programme on antiques, *Going for a Song*.

He is as much at home recounting the deeds of the Dohertys, Perry and Laver as those of Borg, McEnroe and Evert.

Here he tells of the rise to fame of Maureen Connolly, "Little Mo", whom he regarded as the greatest woman lawn tennis player who has ever lived.

MAUREEN CONNOLLY

1952 was a significant year in tennis history. Three all-time greats made their first appearances at Wimbledon — Maureen Connolly ("Little Mo"), Lew Hoad and Ken Rosewall. Little Mo was exceptional. She came, she saw, she conquered — three years running. She then had a tragic riding accident and never played at Wimbledon again.

She was primarily a baseline player, but her accuracy was so unerring and her drives so fierce as they sought out the lines, that she put her opponents under almost continual pressure. She had a huge competitive instinct and at the slightest sign of danger would raise her sights and lessen still further the margin of error. Her drives on either wing became withering and occasionally she put in a delicate surprise drop-shot. When she was in a high mood, the crowd loved to watch her bobbing head, for as soon as a point was finished she immediately turned and marched briskly back to position, her head nodding like that of a foraging chicken. Most lovers of the game give her premier place since 1946 and many feel that she would have raised her game to beat any greats who came before or after her.

Maureen was the most sensational thing to happen to lawn tennis since Suzanne Lenglen. As an eleven-year-old she had been spotted playing on a public court in San Diego, California, by Wilbur Folson, who used to coach youngsters. Wilbur saw the potential in the girl with the curly hair and sparkling eyes and persuaded Mrs Connolly to let him coach Maureen. Almost immediately he made a radical change in her game, getting her to switch from left- to right-handed.

Maureen then came under the guidance of the top tennis coach in Southern California — Eleanor 'Teach' Tennant. Her progress was breathtaking. At thirteen she became the youngest girl to win the National Junior Championships; two years later she was ranked ten in the senior ratings; in August 1951, when only sixteen, she became America's youngest Wightman Cup player, beating Britain's No. 3, Kay Tuckey. The sensations continued, growing in size and in reaction. Nine days later, playing in the American Championships, Maureen knocked out Doris Hart. In the Final against Shirley Fry, sixteen-year-old Maureen took the first set 6/3, lost the second 1/6, and came back to win the decider.

At Wimbledon in her first match she beat Britain's Evelyn Moeller without needing to take off her cardigan. But she did have to struggle in a fourth-round match against attractive Sue Partridge. Here was a player with all the natural graces of beauty and stroke production, but lacking that essential killer instinct, a fault of so many British players. It was a lovely match, with the new phenomenon getting home only by 6/3, 5/7, 7/5. Little Mo also dropped a set in her quarter-final against Thelma Long of Australia. These were the only two sets she was ever to lose at Wimbledon. She reached the Final by beating Shirley Fry.

Champion Doris Hart looked vulnerable in her early matches, and was beaten in the quarter-finals in a long wavering match by Pat Todd, who in turn went out to Louise Brough.

The Final between seventeen-year-old Little Mo and the great Louise, who was conceding some twelve years, was eagerly awaited. Few thought that Maureen, even though she was reigning American champion, could sustain the high pitch she had reached at her first Wimbledon. She did. But how Louise fought to regain the crown she had worn so nobly. At one set down and 2/5 in the second, Louise was 0-40 facing three match-points. She saved them all and a fourth in the following game. But, at the fifth, after a thrilling rally, she was beaten by Little Mo's forehand which flashed across court, past her own. So Maureen, who had been given the nickname 'Little Mo' after the American battleship *Mighty Mo*, had found the range with her big guns to sink all opposition.

From *Wimbledon Centre Court of the Game* by Max Robertson, published by Arthur Barker Ltd.

Russell Braddon

THE FINALISTS

Russell Braddon was born in Australia, and now lives in Britain. He is a biographer, novelist and war historian, and well-known as a broadcaster on discussion programmes.

In this extract from his novel, *The Finalists*, the Wimbledon finalists are Gary King, Australian, and Vissarian Tsarapkin, Russian. They are friends and doubles partners. In the stands an assassin is ready to shoot the Queen and the new champion. In the fifth set both men know that they are fighting for their lives. In the crowded Centre Court the drama is being played out.

From THE FINALISTS

'Something's bugging you.'
Switching to Russian, Tsarapkin said, 'My soldier. Don't look up.'
Replying in Russian, King said, 'I have seen him.'
'That's another soldier. And another sailor. And often they don't watch us playing.'
'Do you think . . . ?'
'I don't know. But all the military people here *asked* to do this work so that they could watch the tennis.'
'At 16-15 we'll talk about it,' King promised. And, reverting to English, 'Till then, let's enjoy ourselves.'

'Oh, this really is glorious stuff,' Maskell observed half way through the next game. 'Tsarapkin is now moving as well as ever and the way he disguised the direction of that last shot, with a very late flick of the wrist, was really quite remarkable.'

'And we're seeing some marvellous returns from Gary King, Dan. Terrific top spin and getting the ball straight to Tsarapkin's feet time after time. Each time, though, this guy Tsarapkin just half volleys it back like it was no trouble at all. They're turning on some really tremendous tennis.'

All of which, along with the rallies so described, was faithfully recorded by Mr Kenton's accomplished technicians, and fed back to the Vision Mixer, who, by inserting a replay of an earlier rally into the recorded version of the match, had managed to maintain the illusion of a live telecast — most of which was, in fact, now not nine but eleven minutes out of date.

'What's happened?' the Commissioner demanded of his subordinates when, at fifteen fourteen, he saw King and Tsarapkin falling about on their chairs with laughter. He and his Think Tank had long since completed their five minute period of watching the tennis in mindless silence; but little had come of it; and now the mood of the game had changed to what looked like a light-hearted badinage and he couldn't understand it.

'Buggered if I know,' Challoner muttered.

'Could they possibly have heard something we didn't?'

'Out there?' Willis queried.

. . . . . .

From Scotland Yard came reports to the Commissioner in his Think Tank advising that the whole of England had been sealed off as effectively as Wimbledon itself. Whoever shot the Queen need not expect to escape. Not *from* England nor *to* anywhere else. The world's police had responded promptly to Scotland Yard's telexed appeals for co-operation, and not simply because of the odium that would attach to any country that failed to apprehend the Queen's assassin.

Somehow the story had leaked overseas and in one country after another editors of newspapers, producers of television programmes and newscasters in radio stations had decided that to use it, when the score in the fifth set — according to Eurovision — was sixteen all, would be neither irresponsible nor unsympathetic. On the contrary, the story was doing more to enhance Britain's reputation abroad than anything since the evacuation of Dunkirk.

In the whole of Europe there was hardly a television set not switched on to bring into homes and bars the drama of two men competing for the right to die with the Queen of

England. In Asia and North America, in Latin America and the Antipodes, the story was the same. In Australia, a million phone calls had roused a million sleeping households and sent them rushing, bleary-eyed, to their sets. Only Africa had remained unmoved.

Nor did this vast foreign audience find the commentaries from London any the less dramatic because they made no mention of the threat to the players and the Queen. That had to be described by local broadcasters speaking over the satellite pictures which showed rather more than the usual number of close-ups of the Queen who was apparently absorbed in the match on the court below her. Russian viewers were unable to make up their minds as to whose courage they admired the most, hers or Tsarapkin's. In every other country there was equal admiration for both.

Only Roddy Weston, in fact, was less than spellbound by Wimbledon's televised story. At sixteen games all, his nerve, unlike Tsarapkin's, had begun to fail.

Maybe, he suddenly thought, it would be better to call everything off. After all, he'd had the law shitting themselves all afternoon. And the Queen had probably only refused to pardon him because the Home Secretary wouldn't let her. Now that she'd been on the receiving end of some punishment for a couple of hours herself, she'd know what it was like and tell her Home Secretary what to do with his advice next time she got a letter from Roddy Weston.

He could write to her tonight, come to think of it. Provided he didn't have her shot this afternoon. Funny that. Now *he* had to decide whether to pardon her.

Actually, it'd be a very smart thing to do, to let her off. Then catch her again at the Royal Gala Performance at Covent Garden at the end of the month. A million quid or she and Sutherland got shot. Christ, they'd cough up before the end of Act One. The Queen herself would insist. Look, she'd say, I'm not going through all that again. I had enough of *that* at Wimbledon.

'You can't miss, Roddy boy!' he told himself. 'They can't stretch an opera out for five hours instead of two like they have this game of tennis. Anyway, it'd be a pity to waste the two hundred nicker you spent on those tickets.'

'Game to Tsarapkin. Tsarapkin leads seventeen games to sixteen in the fifth and final set.'

Weston glowered at the players as they chatted with the effortless intimacy of friends. Then Tsarapkin passed King the letter he'd had Colonel Murray deliver to them, and even though the picture cut instantly to a pretty girl beside the court, it was sufficient momentarily to revive his sagging confidence and stifle his congenital cowardice.

The camera moved off the girl and back to King, who, after a moment's thought, spoke eagerly to Tsarapkin. Maddeningly, Weston could hear King's voice, but understood nothing. Couldn't even identify the Australian vowel sounds. And he had no better luck with Tsarapkin. More chat. Then King said, 'Great! Well? Don't just sit there.'

Infuriated by King's persistent refusal to show fear, Weston swore softly and very obscenely. At least Tsarapkin had revealed gratifying glimpses of tension and despair. But King . . . had Weston not actually *seen* him with that letter in his hand, been able to see it sticking out of the top of his sock right now, it wouldn't have been possible to believe that he had known for hours what lay in store for either him or his mate.

Settling back to watch the tennis, Weston quite forgot that he had been about to telephone *Contact* and say, 'This is Doctor Macdonald. I'm on call and I just want to make sure my bleep is working. Would you page me, please?'

Had he done so, *Contact* would at once have activated Hennessy's second bleep, and Hennessy and Steelman would have known that they were *not* to shoot anyone else. As it was, the games were 21:20, and the match was almost over.

From *The Finalists* by Russell Braddon, published by Michael Joseph Ltd.

Lance Tingay

THE INCOMPARABLE SUZANNE

Lance Tingay began attending the Lawn Tennis championships as a journalist in 1932, and was Lawn Tennis Correspondent to the *Daily Telegraph* from 1952 until his retirement in 1980. He can make compelling narrative from the ups-and-downs of first-class lawn tennis.

He is as much at home in writing about the Dohertys and Suzanne Lenglen as in describing the feats of Hoad and Rosewall and Chris Evert.

THE INCOMPARABLE SUZANNE

Lenglen *père* shadowed his daughter through the early rounds of the women's singles like Svengali with Trilby. The extraordinary high talent of Suzanne was manifest from the start. In the first four rounds she lost a total of only five games and her victims included the 1912 champion, Ethel Larcombe, whom she beat 6-2 6-1. The Californian Elizabeth Ryan, her doubles partner, held her to 6-4 7-5 in the semi-final but she won the All Comer's Final against Phyllis Satterthwaite, a notoriously sticky performer, with ease and so qualified for the challenge round without having lost a set. This was the match that lifted the women's game into the front rank of spectator appeal, a position it never subsequently lost at Wimbledon. It was the triumph of a new generation. It was the psychological breakthrough for the most impressive woman player in the game's history.

The 44 games over which the combat lasted stood in the records as the most rigorous final of the event for more than 50 years. King George V, Queen Mary and their daughter Princess Mary watched it, as entranced as any of the 8000 spectators around the court. Suzanne won by 10-8 4-6 9-7 after twice being within a stroke of losing. She also had two set points against her in the first set.

One may wonder how different might have been the course of lawn-tennis history had this marginal issue turned the other way. Forty years old or no, Mrs Lambert Chambers would have stood as an eight-times singles champion and Suzanne would not have acquired invincibility. One need not be an expert psychologist to realise that the secret of Suzanne's incredible success as a player was her confidence. Whether she could have built a like confidence had she lost and not won at her first appearance at Wimbledon is a matter of speculation.

Be that as it may, she did win, albeit adventurously. She was the more aggressive player in that she volleyed more. None the less she suffered the first set-back in that when leading 5-3 in the first set she missed a set point and, after losing three games in a row, had to save two set balls against her at 5-6. She eventually won the set without falling behind again, taking the last point with a stop volley.

In the second set, a struggle faster and more rigorous than Wimbledon had seen between women, Suzanne, falling behind 1-4, began to show signs of physical distress. Her father fortified her with sugar soaked in brandy and with renewed verve she pulled up to four games all. But the old guard had its triumph after all, Mrs Lambert Chambers secured the next two games for one set all.

In the last set the initial recovery was reversed. Suzanne went to 4-1 and it was the defender who hauled back. Not only that, she went ahead to 5-4, only to lose her service to love. Mrs Lambert Chambers again broke her service to be 6-5 and on her own delivery led 40-15. The pre-war champion thus stood with a double chance to win for the eighth time. On the first match point, Suzanne, in mid court near the net, was lobbed and, in attempting a smash, barely caught the ball with her racket producing a winner that just fell over the net. It was a fluke from the wood! On the second match point Suzanne projected a winning backhand down the line that raised the chalk. Two match points for the defender had come and gone.

Suzanne won her serve to 15 to reach 7-6; Mrs Lambert Chambers squared with the next game but it was near the end and the French challenger finished with a love game against the service. All commentators agreed that it was the finest women's match seen at Wimbledon.

Thus began a career which is unrivalled in its record of

invincibility. Wimbledon's fortunes were not made by the attraction of this *belle laide*, the irresistible player from Picardy, for it was obvious in 1914 and earlier that somewhere bigger than the Worple Road site needed to be found. Her popularity, however, made a move a matter of urgency. Whether they liked it or not Wimbledon's organisers were saddled with a major show-business enterprise, far removed from the gentle sporting occasion with which the tournament had started. Until Suzanne, the women at Wimbledon were tolerated in that arena as a matter of courtesy. With Suzanne it became imperative.

In 1920 and 1921 Suzanne defended her singles in challenge rounds at Worple Road. The crowds who came to watch had no expectation of seeing her crown seriously disputed; they came to see a queen going through the formalities of crowning herself again. Mrs Lambert Chambers was again her rival in 1920 and was in splendid form. She beat the best of the Americans, Molla Mallory, 6-0 6-3 and the ubiquitous Miss Ryan 6-2 6-1 in the final. But in the challenge round she could not raise the spark of the year before or approach the already matured expertise and majestic control of Suzanne. Suzanne lost just three games. The next year she lost only two, this time to Miss Ryan.

Spectators had more value for their money from Suzanne in the doubles. In the women's doubles she and Miss Ryan were dominant for five successive years. In the mixed it was possible to find Suzanne on the losing side. In 1919 she partnered her compatriot H. Laurentz and they lost in the quarter-final to Randolph Lycett and Miss Ryan. A year later she played with the Australian Gerald Patterson and became triple champion. In 1921 she entered again partnered by a Frenchman, André Gobert, but scratched after one round. They did not get on well together and Gobert had an injured ankle anyway. The last match played in the championships at Worple Road was on 3 July 1921. It was the final of the women's doubles in which Suzanne and Miss Ryan overwhelmed Mrs Beamish and Mrs Peacock 6-1 6-2. Appropriately perhaps, it fell to Suzanne to strike the last ball, a smash that allowed no return. It was six days short of 44 years since Spencer Gore or one of his pioneer associates had hit the first ball in a notable series of championship meetings and a pastime had grown into a thriving sport.

At the new venue for the Championships in 1922 at the Church Road ground, when for the first time all events had the defending champions 'playing through', Suzanne set a record of invincibility which surprised no one then but which has not since been equalled. It stands as a record for either sex. Suzanne not only won all three events, singles, doubles and mixed to become triple champion but she did so without yielding a set in any match.

Six rounds of singles, in that wet year, gave her that event by 12 sets to nil, 75 games to 20. Five rounds of women's doubles gave her that by 10 sets to nil, 61 games to 14. Six rounds of mixed were won by 12 sets to nil, 72 games to 25. Miss Ryan was her women's partner, the Australian Pat O'Hara Wood her companion in the mixed. Suzanne played just three advantage sets in 1922, two at 7-5 and one at 8-6. Her average concession of games per set was 1.7.

Her victims in the singles included Kitty McKane, the outstanding British player who later twice won the championship. She had the distinction of forcing Suzanne to a 7-5 set. Miss Ryan in the quarter-final did even better, stretching the champion to 8-6. The final was something of a needle affair, for this was against the American champion Molla Mallory. The previous year Suzanne had made her ill-fated journey to Forest Hills. The controversial drama of what befell her there is not part of Wimbledon's story but it provided the only occasion in Suzanne's post-war career when she was beaten—if, indeed, she can be said to have been beaten. In an unseeded draw she was pitchforked soon after her arrival into her opening match in the US Championships, against, of all opponents, the best in America, the Norwegian-born Mrs Mallory. Suzanne was unwell, lost the first set 6-2 and soon afterwards staggered from the court in default. When they met again nine months later Suzanne needed to rebut the American charge that she was a 'quitter' and inferior to Mrs Mallory.

The Frenchwoman took uncompromising revenge after a match that was dramatic in its brevity and the Wagnerian quality of its setting. Because of rain it did not start until one minute past seven in the evening. At 7.26 Suzanne was the winner by 6-2 6-0 after ruthless exploitation of the most vigorous pace and control from the back of the court.

A year later, Suzanne went through the singles with never a set going beyond nine games. The most games she lost were those in the final; this was against Miss McKane and the score was 6-2 6-2! The women's doubles was similarly formal, Miss Ryan again being her partner, and if the two events be taken together the French triumph was taking 22 sets for the average loss of less than 1.3 games. But there was no triple championship that year. Partnered by the Belgian, J. Washer, she lost to Lycett and Miss Ryan in the semi-final of the mixed.

Her start in the 1924 Wimbledon Championships was meteoric enough to promise the most overwhelming win of all time. In the singles it was 6-0 6-0 in both the first and second rounds. Then it was 6-0 6-0 again, this remarkably because it was against Hazel Wightman, the former US champion. Suzanne could claim another unique record in this; she took half a dozen love sets in sequence. With no pressure she and Miss Ryan won two rounds of the women's doubles and with Jean Borotra three rounds of the mixed. But she had had an attack of jaundice in the spring and it was clear that her recovery was not complete. She had difficulty in winning her quarter-final against Miss Ryan. She survived merely by 6-2 6-8 6-4. The loss of the set was noteworthy. Certainly Miss Ryan had never played better and Miss Ryan, probably more than anyone, could play the Frenchwoman with a measure of confidence. Suzanne, having pushed herself to the limit to survive, retired sick from the meeting.

The gap thus opened brought a revival of British fame. Kitty McKane, the best of the British, had the walkover against Suzanne and met an American of 18 in the final. This was Helen Wills, later to be Helen Wills Moody and, quantitatively, the greatest of all Wimbledon singles champions. The previous autumn she won the US singles for the first time. Her progress to the final was, more or less, as overwhelming as Suzanne had achieved in the past. After five matches she was one step short of the title having dropped only eleven games in five contests.

One of the most famous women's matches of all time was in 1926 at Cannes when Suzanne Lenglen beat Helen Wills 6-3 8-6. It was the only clash between the two most formidable players in the history of the women's game. But for Suzanne's illness their meeting would have been two years earlier in the final at Wimbledon—or, at least—such is reasonable to assume. That it never came about was regrettable but none the less Suzanne's absence brought a spectacular climax to the women's championships. It would have been an even more piquant contest at the time had spectators known that they were watching the only occasion Miss Wills was to lose in singles at Wimbledon. It was a staunch win for Kitty McKane and, uncharacteristically, the American let slip a winning lead. Miss McKane lost the first set 4-6, trailed 1-4 and was four times within a point of falling to 1-5 in the second,

Lawn Tennis

before former British glories were reasserted with a victory by 4-6 6-4 6-4. Wimbledon did not see the remarkable Miss Wills for another three years.

In 1925, however, Suzanne was seen with a vengeance. As in 1922 she became triple champion, gaining the women's doubles for the sixth time with Miss Ryan and the mixed, this time with Borotra, for the third. But she was a shade less invincible than in 1922, for she lost a set in the semi-final of the mixed. None the less, her singles record was the most shattering.

She was unlucky in the draw in that nearly all the best players were in her half—Wimbledon was still a year short of having full merit seeding. In her first match Suzanne beat Miss Ryan, who was ranked fourth best in the world that year, by 6-2 6-0. In the next she beat Elsie Goldsack, one of the leading British women, 6-1 6-0. Then she beat Mrs Beamish, British Wightman Cup player, 6-0 6-0. Next, this being the semi-final, she met the title holder Kitty McKane. Suzanne won 6-0 6-0. The finalist was another British player, Joan Fry, from Staffordshire. That was an astonishing story in itself, for Miss Fry, competing for the first time at the age of 19, valiantly burst her way through to the last match despite a county selection committee that had omitted her earlier in the year. Miss Fry was beaten 6-2 6-0.

The record, then, for the impeccable Suzanne was five matches won, ten sets won, for the entire loss of five games. She conceded two games in two matches, one in another and that was all. Miss McKane, whom she whitewashed, was, that year, ranked third best player in the world.

This was Suzanne Lenglen's last championship, for events in 1926 were curious and dramatic. The singles she had taken six times in seven years, the doubles six times also, all with Miss Ryan. The mixed she had won three times, so all in all Suzanne Lenglen recorded her Wimbledon immortality with a total of fifteen championships. Her scores in the singles finals stress her breathtaking superiority:

1919 beat Mrs Lambert Chambers 10-8 4-6 9-7
     after which no rival got near
1920 beat Mrs Lambert Chambers 6-3 6-0
1921 beat Miss Ryan 6-2 6-0
1922 beat Mrs Mallory 6-2 6-0
1923 beat Miss McKane 6-2 6-2
1925 beat Miss Fry 6-2 6-0

The events of 1926, which brought an end to the incredible amateur career of Suzanne Lenglen, should perhaps be put in focus by the happenings which preceded her ill-fated swan song. There was the backcloth of her one-sided victory of the year before. On the Riviera circuit the long-awaited clash between Suzanne and the new American star, Helen Wills, had at last come about when, at Cannes, the Frenchwoman won by 6-3, 8-6. Then, in the French Championships held in those days at St Cloud, Miss Wills had withdrawn with appendicitis. Here Suzanne surpassed her 1925 Wimbledon effort. She took the singles for the total loss of only four games in five matches, Miss Fry having the distinction of winning three of them in the semi-final.

Thus when Suzanne began her Wimbledon challenge in 1926 it was to a background of utter invincibility and expectation of overwhelming success. She was more than a dynamic and irresistible player. She was, *par excellence*, a prima donna, her fame and prestige extending far beyond the sporting world.

This, though, was a year when the meeting was heightened by other out of the ordinary happenings. It was celebrated as Jubilee Year with the assemblage of as many old champions as could be mustered; the Royal patronage at the commemorative ceremonies on the Centre Court was the occasion of special interest and excitement. There was more stress on Wimbledon's status as an event than on individual personality. Suzanne Lenglen proved, on this occasion, to be an embarrassment that was echoed in accounts recorded by those who shared in them.

Suzanne's 'walk out' from the Championships that year had its roots in a conflict between two strong personalities, that of Suzanne herself, and Frank Burrow, the referee. Burrow, who was certainly an efficient referee, was equally certainly an authoritarian in his office. He was not the sort of referee any player could 'push around'. Equally Suzanne was hardly a player who could be 'pushed around'. Her status in the championships was such that it had become the custom for one of the executives to escort her each day to the referee's office to be told the times she would be required on the morrow. In 1926 after she had beaten the American Mary Browne in the opening round (by 6-2 6-3) on the first Tuesday, this was not done. She left without getting in touch with Burrow. He, in due course, made out his order of play, putting Suzanne to play her second round singles on the Centre Court at two o'clock with a doubles later.

Queen Mary was in the Royal Box, doubtless as avid to see

Lawn Tennis

the incomparable Suzanne in action as everyone else. There was no Suzanne! She arrived at the ground at 3.30. So far as the Wimbledon executive was concerned she was an absentee and liable to be scratched from the singles.

Suzanne herself had learned from her partner, Didi Vlasto, that morning, but only that morning, that she was wanted for a singles. In vain she tried to telephone Wimbledon to tell them she wished only to play the doubles. She settled in the end for ringing her compatriot Toto Brugnon and asked him to pass on the message. This he did in due course but it seems the message was not passed to Burrow. Suzanne, arriving in what she thought was good time for just one doubles match, found herself treated not with the usual courtesy but summoned before the committee and reprimanded for being late. This was not the sort of treatment a prima donna was accustomed to; she retreated to the dressing room in hysterics.

From *100 Years of Wimbledon* by Lance Tingay, published by Guinness Superlatives Ltd.

Acknowledgments

The Editor and Publishers would like to thank the following for their kind permission to reproduce the extracts in this book:

Adam and Charles Black Publishers for the extract from Bernard Darwin: "The Links of Eiderdown" from *Mostly Golf*, edited by Peter Ryde.
Cassell Ltd for Rex Bellamy: "The Greatest Tennis Show on Earth" from *The Tennis Set* by Rex Bellamy; and for Henry Longhurst: "The Greatest Tournament in the World" from *Never On Weekdays* by Henry Longhurst.
Colin Cowdrey and *Country Life* for "Hambledon Interlude" (*Country Life*, 18 August 1977).
The Cricketer Ltd and Hutchinson & Co Ltd for the extract from Ian Peebles: *Woolley: The Pride of Kent*.
The *Daily Telegraph* for Harold Pinter: "Memories of Cricket" from the *Daily Telegraph Magazine* (16 May 1969).
Epworth, Methodist Publishing House, for Ronald Mason: "An Over of O'Reilly's" from *Sing all a green willow*.
Eyre & Spottiswoode Ltd for Hugh McIlvanney: "The Brazilians" from *World Cup '70*, edited by Hugh McIlvanney and Arthur Hopcraft.
John Farquharson Ltd for Brian Glanville: "World Cup Final '66".
Geoffrey Green, c/o David Higham Associates Ltd, for "Lightning Strikes in Turin" from *Great Moments in Sport: Soccer* by Geoffrey Green, published by Pelham Books Ltd.
Michael Green, c/o Curtis Brown, for "K is for Kicker" from *Michael Green's Rugby Alphabet*, published by Pelham Books Ltd.
The *Guardian* for John Arlott: "When Laker walked tall on Park Avenue" (23 April 1980); Alistair Cooke: "Jacklin Wins U.S. Open" (22 June 1970); David Frost: "Barry John's Three Gifts" (9 May 1972); David Gray: "The Springtime of a Great Talent" (3 July 1971); Carwyn James: "A young romantic rediscovers some of his old poetry" (14 March 1975); Pat Ward-Thomas: "Nine Holes with Jack Nicklaus" (1 May 1968) and "The Agony of the First Hole at St Andrews" (15 May 1969).
Guinness Superlatives Ltd for Lance Tingay: "The Incomparable Suzanne" from *100 Years of Wimbledon* by Lance Tingay.

William Heinemann Ltd for Stephen Potter: "Handicap Types" from *The Complete Golf Gamesmanship* by Stephen Potter.

Hodder & Stoughton Ltd for Geoffrey Moorhouse: "The Roses Match" from *The Best Loved Game* by Geoffrey Moorhouse (1979).

Arthur Hopcraft, c/o A. P. Watt Ltd, for "Eulogy" from *The Football Man* by Arthur Hopcraft, published by William Collins Ltd.

Michael Joseph Ltd for the extract from Russell Braddon: *The Finalists*; for Richard Llewellyn: "On the Mound" from *How Green Was My Valley* by Richard Llewellyn; and for Alun Richards: "The Template" from *A Touch of Glory* by Alun Richards.

Irene Josephy for John Moynihan: "Park Shooting" from *Park Football*, published by Pelham Books Ltd.

London Magazine Editions for the extract from J. L. Carr: *How Steeple Sinderby Wanderers Won the F.A.Cup*.

William Luscombe, Mitchell Beazley London Ltd, for the extract from David Irvine: *The Joy of Rugby*.

The *Observer* for Peter Dobereiner: "Fading into Stardom" (11 January 1981) and "The Flowering of a Fantasy" (15 March 1981).

Stanley Paul Ltd for Michael Parkinson: "Webb" from *Cricket Mad* by Michael Parkinson.

Pelham Books Ltd for J. B. G. Thomas: "Jarrett's Match" from *Great Moments in Sport* by J. B. G. Thomas.

Penguin Books Ltd for the extract from David Storey: *This Sporting Life* (pages 246-249).

Max Robertson for "Maureen Connolly" from *Wimbledon Centre Court of the Game*.

The Scottish Academic Press for Pat Ward-Thomas: "Homage to a Peerless Golfer" from *The Royal and Ancient* by Pat Ward-Thomas.

Souvenir Press Ltd, for Sir Neville Cardus: "George Gunn", pages 132-135 of *Cardus on Cricket*.

The *Times* for Alan Gibson: "A batting machine they called 'The Croucher' " (18 May 1974); Geoffrey Green: "One Hundred Years of Cup Magic" (6 May 1972) and Christmas Card Jogs a Brazilian Memory" (23 December 1967).

The Estate of P. G. Wodehouse and the Hutchinson Group Ltd, c/o A. P. Watt Ltd, for the extract from P. G. Wodehouse: "Rodney Fails to Qualify" from *The Golf Omnibus* by P. G. Wodehouse.

Index of Authors

Arlott, John 15
Bellamy, Rex 149
Braddon, Russell 156
Cardus, Sir Neville 11
Carr, J. L. 47
Cooke, Alistair 122
Cowdrey, Colin 28
Darwin, Bernard 140
Dobereiner, Peter 116
Frost, David 82
Gibson, Alan 39
Glanville, Brian 50
Gray, David 145
Green, Geoffrey 64
Green, Michael 84
Hopcraft, Arthur 60
Irvine, David 75
James, Carwyn 78, 96

Llewellyn, Richard 91
Longhurst, Henry 125
Mason, Ronald 24
McIlvanney, Hugh 56
Moorhouse, Geoffrey 42
Moynihan, John 71
Parkinson, Michael 31
Peebles, Ian 35
Pinter, Harold 20
Potter, Stephen 128
Richards, Alun 94
Robertson, Max 153
Storey, David 101
Thomas, J. B. G. 87
Tingay, Lance 160
Ward-Thomas, Pat 107
Wodehouse, P. G. 132

Index of Titles

The Agony of the First Hole at St Andrews 111
Barry John's Three Gifts 82
A batting machine they called 'The Croucher' 39
The Brazilians 56
Christmas Card Jogs a Brazilian Memory 67
Eulogy 60
Fading into Stardom 116
From *The Finalists* 156
The Flowering of a Fantasy 119
George Gunn 11
The Greatest Tennis Show on Earth 149
The Greatest Tournament in the World 125
Hambledon Interlude 28
Handicap Types 128
Homage to a Peerless Golfer 113
From *How Steeple Sinderby Wanderers Won the F.A.Cup* 47
The Incomparable Suzanne 160
Jacklin Wins U.S. Open 122
Jarrett's Match 87
From *The Joy of Rugby* 75
K is for Kicker 84
Lightning Strikes in Turin 69
The Links of Eiderdown 140
Maureen Connolly 153
Memories of Cricket 20
Nine Holes with Jack Nicklaus 107
On the Mound 91
One Hundred Years of Cup Magic 64
An Over of O'Reilly's 24
Park Shooting 71
From "Rodney Fails to Qualify" 132
The Roses Match 42
The Springtime of a Great Talent 145
The Template 94
From *This Sporting Life* 101
Webb 31
When Laker walked tall on Park Avenue 15
From *Woolley: The Pride of Kent* 35
World Cup Final '66 50
A young romantic rediscovers some of his old poetry 78